Marital
Equality

**SAGE SERIES ON
CLOSE RELATIONSHIPS**

Series Editors
Clyde Hendrick, Ph.D., and
Susan S. Hendrick, Ph.D.

In this series...

Marital Equality

Its Relationship to
the Well-Being of
Husbands and Wives

Janice M. Steil

Sage
Series
on Close
Relationships

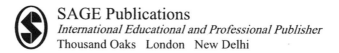

SAGE Publications
International Educational and Professional Publisher
Thousand Oaks   London   New Delhi

For information:

 SAGE Publications, Inc.
2455 Teller Road
Thousand Oaks, California 91320
E-mail: order@sagepub.com

SAGE Publications Ltd.
6 Bonhill Street
London EC2A 4PU
United Kingdom

SAGE Publications India Pvt. Ltd.
M-32 Market
Greater Kailash I
New Delhi 110 048 India

Printed in the United States of America

Library of Congress Cataloging-in-Publication Data

Steil, Janice M. Ingham, 1941-
   Marital equality: Its relationship to the well-being of
husbands and wives / Janice M. Steil.
      p. cm.—(Sage series on close relationships)
   Includes bibliographical references (p.) and index.
   ISBN 0-8039-5250-3 (cloth : acid-free paper).—
ISBN 0-8039-5251-1 (pbk. : acid-free paper)
   1. Marriage—United States—Psychological aspects. 2. Married
people—United States—Psychology. 3. Equality—United States—
Psychological aspects. 4. Sex differences (Psychology)—United States.
5. Sex role—United States. I. Title. II. Series.
HQ536.S735 1997
306.81—dc21   97-4797

97 98 99 00 01 02 03 10 9 8 7 6 5 4 3 2 1

Acquiring Editor: C. Terry Hendrix
Editorial Assistant: Dale Mary Grenfell
Production Editor: Sanford Robinson
Production Assistant: Lynn Miyata
Typesetter/Designer: Marion Warren
Cover Designer: Candice Harman
Print Buyer: Anna Chin

Contents

Series Editors' Introduction

When we first began our work on love attitudes more than a decade ago, we did not know what to call our research area. In some ways it represented an extension of earlier work in interpersonal attraction. Most of our scholarly models were psychologists (though sociologists had long been deeply involved in the areas of courtship and marriage), yet we sometimes felt as if our work had no professional "home." That has all changed. Our research not only has a home but also has an extended family, and the family is composed of relationship researchers. During the past decade, the discipline of close relationships (also called personal relationships and intimate relationships) has emerged, developed, and flourished.

Two aspects of close relationships research should be noted. The first is its rapid growth, resulting in numerous books, journals, handbooks, book series, and professional organizations. As fast as the field grows, the demand for even more research and knowledge seems to be ever increasing. Questions about close, personal relationships still far exceed answers. The second noteworthy aspect of the new discipline of close relationships is its interdisciplinary nature. The field owes its vitality to scholars from communications, family studies and human development, psychology (clinical, counseling, developmental, social), sociology, and other disciplines, such as nursing and social work. This interdisciplinary wellspring is what gives close relationships research its diversity and richness, qualities that we hope to achieve in the current series.

The Sage Series on Close Relationships is designed to acquaint diverse readers with the most up-to-date information about various topics in close relationships theory and research. Each volume in the series covers a particular topic or theme in one area of close relationships. Each book reviews the particular topic area, describes contemporary research in the area (including the authors' own work, where appropriate), and offers some suggestions for interesting research questions or real-world applications related to the topic. The volumes are designed to be appropriate for students and professionals in communications, family studies, psychology, sociology, and social work, among others. A basic assumption of the series is that the broad panorama of close relationships can best be portrayed by authors from multiple disciplines, so the series cannot be "captured" by any single disciplinary bias.

The interrelationships among gender, power, and satisfaction in marriage have often appeared as a tangled web. Who has the power in the family, and what kind? Why do women appear to "settle for" less power? Does male entitlement exist?

In the current volume, *Marital Equality: Its Relationship to the Well-Being of Husbands and Wives,* Janice M. Steil has untangled this web. Systematically employing decades of empirical findings to examine the various strands, Steil traces research from Jesse Bernard's groundbreaking work in the 1970s to the most recent examinations of the topic. Issues such as full-time homemaking versus paid work, links between well-being and power, relationship equality and equity, intimacy, and the difficulties of achieving true relationship equality are all untangled and addressed.

Women have become more and more involved in society's paid work and thus in the family's financial sustenance, but men as a group have not achieved similar involvement in the family's emotional sustenance. Why has that occurred, how has it been maintained, and what might "equality" look like in an intimate relationship such as marriage? These issues and more are discussed by Steil in what might be a groundbreaking book of the 1990s.

CLYDE HENDRICK
SUSAN S. HENDRICK
SERIES EDITORS

*To Justin, Alexis, and their relationships
in the second millennium.*

Preface

During the time that I have been working on this book, I have often been asked in social situations what the book is about. In the beginning, I responded that it was a book about marital equality. I was struck by the varied reactions this response evoked. Young unmarried women often suggested that equality was a problem of my generation, not theirs. Married women, in contrast, who did tend to be older, responded with instant understanding but universal skepticism that marital equality could ever be achieved. Men's responses were much more varied. A few of the younger men responded with sincere interest and with stories of their personal struggles of trying to be supportive of their wives and their wives' careers. Other men responded with stiffened shoulders and straightened spines, and some asked apprehensively, "Are you going to be mean to men?"

To the young women, I often replied with descriptions of the findings of my own studies of high-achieving dual-career women in their early 30s, the majority of whom were married to men who endorsed equality, but most of whom had failed to achieve those egalitarian ideals once their children were born. I listened with interest to the men who told of their personal struggles to support their wives' careers. The men with the stiffened spines and straightened shoulders usually changed the subject. Few of them will probably ever read this book. If any do, however, I hope they will find their apprehensions unfounded.

In more recent times, when asked what the book is about, I say it's about relationships and the conditions under which relationships are equally beneficial for women and for men. For though my interest in the issues of equality came from my own experiences as a woman, a wife, and a mother struggling to pursue her work in the context of few societal supports, I believe that unequal relationships are costly for men and for women, and that men, women, and families will all benefit from relationships based on more equal sharing.

So what *is* this book about? This is a book about adult close relationships. But it is a book with a particular focus. Although it seeks to identify the relationship characteristics that contribute to the psychological well-being of women and men, the focus throughout is primarily on one relationship type, heterosexual marriage. Within the context of that focus, it suggests that the time of greatest relationship dissatisfaction and poorest well-being, especially for women, occurs when there are young children in the home. Yet there is no attempt to systematically survey the well-being of husbands and wives across the lifespan of their relationship. Furthermore, and consistent with the focus of the book, I suggest that the decrements in women's psychological well-being emanate less from the presence of children, per se, than from the inequality of relationships that becomes particularly salient, even among the most egalitarian couples, when children are young.

I have made an explicit effort throughout to consider the relevance of the issues to African American and other minority populations. The fact is, however, that my own work and that of the field is disproportionately based on the study of nonminority samples. This is an important limitation of the work in this area. Over 90% of the population still marries at some time in their life, but there is a growing racial gap in the likelihood of ever marrying. In 1994, 65% of white and Hispanic men age 18 and over were currently married, compared to only 46% of black men. Black women were less likely to be currently married than any other group. Only 40% of black women were married, compared to almost 61% of white and Hispanic women.

Black marriages are generally perceived as more egalitarian than white marriages, but throughout the book I suggest that this assertion is based on limited empirical support. Black women and men are more likely than their white counterparts to view women's paid employment as consistent with the mothering role, but black women are no less likely than white women to emphasize the importance of husbands as providers and wives as primarily responsible for the care of the home and the children. Furthermore, what limited evidence there is suggests that black women benefit less from marriage than any other group. Clearly there is much to be understood here.

The achievement of the conditions under which relationships are equally beneficial to women, men, and their children is influenced by a number of sociostructural, cultural, relational, and individual factors. Relationships simultaneously reflect and produce the values of the larger society. Crosby (1991) suggests that two of the societal impediments to the achievement of equality are sexism and individualism. *Sexism*, according to Crosby, engenders the perception that women's jobs are secondary, and that women work by permission, not by right. Sexism results in women doing lots of work but having little power at home. *Individualism* fosters the presumption that children must be raised exclusively within the confines of the isolated nuclear family. Individualism also supports the privacy of relationships. To talk about one's relationship difficulties and dissatisfactions is to betray one's partner and the sanctity of the relationship. One of the consequences of this is the tendency to minimize the effect of sociostructural factors, such as the lack of child care and workplace flexibility, that increase relationship stress when children are young.

Throughout the book, I attempt to integrate some of the individual and cultural factors that play a role in maintaining inequality. But the emphasis throughout is primarily on relationships. My hope is that presenting the accumulated evidence of what is normative will minimize the tendency of women to blame themselves or their partners, will awaken men to the pervasiveness and the consequences of the problem, and will lead men and women together to effect societal and relationship change.

Finally, and in a somewhat related vein, the majority of the chapters reflect the historical evolution of one particular aspect of relationship research sometimes referred to as *gender justice*. One aspect of this work is a disproportionate emphasis on the costs of inequality for women, thereby neglecting the costs of inequality to men. Women have been uniquely disadvantaged, and women have disproportionately born the burden of initiating and enforcing change. But for change to be achieved, men must become full partners in the struggle. Ultimately, then, the problem of relationship inequality must be redefined as a problem not only for women but for men, relationships, and society. One of the ways to achieve this is to make the focus of research more symmetrical: to show the costs that inequality inflicts on the advantaged and the disadvantaged and the benefits of equality to both.

Although I did not consciously intend it, at some point in the writing of this book I realized that it was taking a professionally autobiographical form. That is, the ordering of the chapters and the questions they addressed paralleled the ordering of the questions as they evolved in my own research. Here, I make this evolution explicit.

As a graduate student in social psychology in the late '70s, I worked with Morton Deutsch, and through my work with him, I became interested in the psychology of justice. My early research looked at three issues: (a) the conditions under which victims of discriminatory systems deny that they are disadvantaged; (b) the conditions under which the disadvantaged acknowledge a discriminatory system and seek change; and (c) the conditions under which third-party persons, who are not the agents of a discriminatory system but benefit from it, act on behalf of the disadvantaged.

After completing my degree and accepting an assistant professorship in a program in clinical psychology at the Derner Institute of Advanced Psychological Studies at Adelphi, I was asked to write a review chapter for the *Handbook of Family and Marital Therapy*. As a nonclinician, I was a little surprised to be asked, but as an untenured junior faculty member, I didn't want to seem unwilling. So I proposed a chapter review of the literature on family power.

In the course of this work I read *The Future of Marriage* by the late Jessie Bernard and was introduced to her concept of the "his" and "her" marriage that is now the underlying focus of this book. (Bernard's thesis and her work are reported in more detail in Chapter 1.) In its most succinct form, Bernard, after conducting a secondary analysis of a number of studies, concluded that there are two marriages in every marriage—"his" and "hers," and his is better than hers. Married women, she found, exhibited higher levels of psychological distress, "suffer[ed] far greater mental health hazards and present[ed] a far worse clinical picture" than married men (Bernard, 1982, p. 28).

Reflecting the demographics of the 1960s, when much of the original data was collected, and the early 1970s, when the book was first published, Bernard proposed that the gender differences in well-being among the married were attributable to differences in women's and men's social roles. She, and others, focused on the psychological costs of "housewifery" and the lack of outside sources of gratification when women are unemployed.

In reviewing the literature for the *Handbook* chapter, I proposed a variation on her hypothesis. Integrating what until then had been two discrete bodies of literature, that on family power and that on psychological well-being, I hypothesized that the differences in husbands' and wives' well-being might best be understood as a reflection of the differences in husbands' and wives' marital power. The review of these literatures suggested that the patterns of well-being among the married closely paralleled the distribution of power between husbands and wives. Employed husbands, it seemed, had the greatest say in their marriages and scored highest on measures of well-being. Unemployed homemakers had the least decision-making say in their marriages and scored lowest on measures of well-being. Employed wives scored somewhere between employed husbands and unemployed wives on both.

A few years later, in a collaborative study with Beth Turetsky, I undertook one of the early direct tests of the relationship between marital power and psychological well-being among a sample of 815 dual-earner couples. The findings of that study, as those of several others conducted at that time, provided partial support for the hypothesis that women's and men's level of influence in their marriage is directly related to well-being. But the findings also raised as many questions as they answered. The findings showed, for example, that employed women suffered a decline in influence when they had children but didn't explain why. The findings also suggested that resources, such as income and income relative to one's spouse, worked differently for women than for men and for mothers compared to nonmothers; but again, they didn't explain why. The findings of that and subsequent studies also showed that neither income nor income relative to one's spouse was the best predictor of partners' influence levels. Contrary, perhaps, to expectation, the single best predictor of marital influence was not any of the income variables but rather husbands' and wives' perceptions of the importance of their own careers relative to their spouses' careers. But it was unclear what perceived job importance was really measuring.

Finally, the findings showed that for some of the influence measures, such as say in decision making, equality was associated with greater well-being. Also consistent with that hypothesis, the more that husbands were involved in child care, the less psychological symptomatology their wives reported. But for other measures the findings were not always consistent with the hypotheses. Contrary to hypothesis, the more that husbands were involved in the work of the home, the *more* symptomatology wives reported. The picture, it seemed, was more complicated than one might originally have thought.

Since the publication of Bernard's book, the demographics of American families have changed dramatically. Fifty-six percent of mothers with children under the age of 6 are now employed, and women now comprise almost half (46%) of the paid labor force. During this same period, the literature on relationships and well-being has burgeoned. There is now considerable evidence showing that the way influence is distributed in a relationship is important for the well-being of the partners. Findings reported in Chapters 3 and 4 show that inequality is costly to the less powerful partner in terms of increased dependency, lowered self-esteem, and more frequent feelings of hostility and depression. Inequality is costly to the more powerful partner in terms of decreased openness, loss of intimacy, and decreased relationship satisfaction. Equality, in contrast, is associated with greater relationship satisfaction, more direct and mutual modes of influence, less depression, especially for women, and increased intimacy for both partners.

Yet relationships continue to be unequal. Wives' roles have expanded at an astonishing rate, but husbands' roles have not. The vast majority of married women are now in the paid labor force, but women still bear a disproportionate responsibility for the work of relationships, of the home, and the children. "His" marriage continues to be better than "hers." Yet studies consistently show that wives are not proportionately aggrieved. Why? And if equality is indeed beneficial to men, to women, and to the relationships they share, then why has there been so little change? Why is equality so difficult to achieve?

In some ways, then, the research questions have come full circle. One must once again ask, why is it that the disadvantaged do not seem proportionately aggrieved? What are the conditions under which the advantaged will act on behalf of the disadvantaged? And why is change so difficult to achieve?

❧ Overview of the Chapters

This book begins with a review in Chapter 1 of Bernard's thesis and the alternative explanations and subsequent studies sparked by her work. Chapter 2 reviews and integrates the findings from the early literature, assessing the extent to which the social roles hypothesis explains the gender differences in well-being. Reflecting the gender ideologies of the 1970s, many of the early studies were carried out with an expectation that paid employment would be detrimental to women's well-being. Instead, studies show that employed women often fare better and never fare worse than full-time homemakers. Yet they seldom fare as well as employed husbands. Independent of race and class, the benefits of paid employment are linked not only to the characteristics of a woman's work environment but also to the quality of her parental and marital relationships. Yet wives receive less instrumental and emotional support from their spouses than do husbands. Chapter 3 presents the literature from the 1980s to the present on the relationship between partners' level of relationship power and their psychological well-being. The consistencies and the inconsistencies in the findings raise a number of questions about the psychological legacy of internalized gender roles for even the most egalitarian couples. Chapter 4 reviews the diverse, multidisciplinary literature on relationship equality and asks, how should equality be defined? How should it be measured? Does equality matter? Chapter 5 considers the intimacy literature. There is growing evidence that the level and quality of relationship intimacy is strongly related to husbands' and wives' well-being. Some scholars have suggested that mature intimacy can develop only in a context of equality yet, as this chapter shows, there are gendered differences in the work of intimacy given and intimacy received. The final chapter, Chapter 6, focuses on the "his" and "her" marriage of the 1990s. The changing demographics of relationships are presented with a special look at the puzzling question of the reasons for the racial difference in the likelihood of marrying. The chapter and the book conclude by highlighting several of the factors I believe are crucial to an understanding of why relationship equality is so difficult to achieve. Women disproportionately bear the burden of initiating and enforcing change. Ironically, however, women's role as change agent conflicts with their role as nurturer and relationship maintainer. Furthermore, the motivation to seek change requires a perception of inequality as unfair, but women are impeded in their perceptions of inequality as unfair by gender differences in the sense of entitlement. Although the costs of initiating change should not be minimized, neither should the rewards. More equal relationships benefit men and women and allow women and men together the opportunity to enjoy the more intimate relationships so important to both husbands' and wives' well-being.

Acknowledgments

I would like to express my sincere thanks to the many who have contributed to this endeavor. Students in the social psychology classes at the Derner Institute read and commented in the most constructive and thoughtful ways on different chapters of this book in their various states of evolution. Over the years, the students in my research group have been very special to me and made my years at Derner especially rewarding. I love them all and many of the chapters include descriptions of studies that we have done together.

I have had some wonderful T.A.s who have helped with sundry but important tasks. Most recently Vanessa McGann helped in the most good-spirited and conscientious way with all the references. Susan Rosenbluth, a former member of the research group, has been especially supportive through the years and with this book, as has Diane Sholomskas.

The ideas for this book came together while I was writing a chapter for another book, edited by Mel Lerner and Gerald Mikula. At that time Judy Worell, Faye Crosby, and Fran Deutsch made extremely thoughtful and insightful comments. I am appreciative of their many years of friendship and support.

I would also like to thank my family. My daughter, Alexis, always managed to leave supportive messages on my computer while putting up with my working absences. My son, Justin, in my lowest moment, revived the manuscript when my computer was destroyed by a torrential leak in our apartment. My mother helped out, once again, on short notice, as she had years before, when I needed time to finish. Finally, my thanks to my husband, Peter, for his unwavering confidence.

1

His and Her Marriage
Research From the 1970s

There are two marriages . . . in every marital union, his and hers.
And his . . . is better than hers.

Bernard, 1982, p. 14.

In 1972[1], Jessie Bernard published a book in which she examined the relationship between sex (female or male), marital status (never married, married, widowed, or divorced), and a number of measures of well-being. The measures of well-being were essentially of two types. The first type measured subjective well-being. These measures included assessments of men's and women's self-reported satisfaction and happiness with their marriages and their lives. The second type measured psychological symptomatology. These included assessments of the prevalence of symptoms of psychological distress, such as nervousness, fainting, headaches, trembling hands, and more severe disorders, such as depression,

1

severe neurotic symptoms, and phobic tendencies.[2] On the basis of this data, Bernard (1982) concluded that "there are two marriages . . . in every marital union, his and hers. And his . . . is better than hers" (p. 14).

Bernard reached these conclusions after making three types of comparisons. On each of the well-being measures she compared (a) married men with married women, (b) never-married men with never-married women, and (c) the married with the never-married. When she compared the well-being of married men with never-married men, she found that the married were less likely to show serious symptoms of psychological distress and were less likely to suffer mental health impairments than those who were never married. On the average, married men also lived longer, experienced greater career success, and were less likely to be involved in crime than men who were never married. Among men, then, the married fared far better than the never married. When Bernard compared married women with never-married women, she again found that the married generally fared better than the never married. Overall, then, marriage seemed to have a beneficial effect both for women and men.

Next, Bernard compared married men with married women on each of the well-being measures. Married women exhibited higher levels of psychological distress, "suffer[ed] far greater mental health hazards and present[ed] a far worse clinical picture" than married men (Bernard, 1982, p. 28). Married women were more likely to have felt that they were about to have a nervous breakdown; more likely to experience psychological and physical anxiety (nervousness and insomnia, headaches and heart palpitations); and showed more phobic reactions, more depression, and more passivity than married men. Among the married, women did not fare as well as men.

Bernard then compared the well-being of men and women who had never married. Among the never married, the pattern was reversed. Never-married men were more likely to show health impairments than never-married women. They were more depressed and passive; showed more neurotic and antisocial tendencies, and were more likely to have felt they were about to have a nervous breakdown and to experience psychological anxiety. Only among the married, then, did women show more symptomatology than men. Marriage, it seems, is good for both men and women but better for men. Why?

Bernard explained the well-being differences among the married in terms of the structural strains that the institution of marriage imposes on wives, particularly housewives. She offered a social roles explanation that focused particularly on the psychological costs of housewifery and the lack of outside sources of gratification when women are unemployed. The role of housewife, she argued, is socially isolating, unstructured, subject to unceasing demands, and makes women ill.

Bernard's work generated considerable controversy. Some questioned the extent to which marriage is indeed beneficial, and others questioned the extent to which marriage is really more beneficial for men than for women.

≈ The Protective Effect of Marriage

Among those who asked whether or not marriage is beneficial, some explained the well-being differences between the married and the never married in terms of social selectivity. The social selectivity position maintains that people who are emotionally unstable or physically disabled are less able to marry, and, if they do get married, they are less able to stay married. Thus, it is not that marriage is beneficial to well-being, but that those who are the least well, both mentally and physically, are least able to get married. Others argued that the selection interpretation is generally made by those who study people with severe impairments. Indeed, reviews of the literature suggest that although the selectivity hypothesis may be appropriate for the severely impaired, it does not explain the relationship between marital status and mental health in the normal population (Gove, Hughes, & Style, 1983; Mastekaasa, 1995).

Pearlin and Johnson (1977) questioned the extent to which the married might enjoy higher levels of psychological well-being not because marriage itself is particularly beneficial, but simply because the married are less likely to experience serious life stresses, such as economic hardship and social isolation. To assess the prevalence of economic hardship, they asked respondents: How

often does it happen that you do not have enough money to afford
(1) the kind of food you (your family) should have? (2) the kind of
medical care you (your family) should have? (3) the kind of cloth-
ing you (your family) should have? Social isolation was defined
in terms of social networks rather than intimacy (see Chapter 5)
and examined in terms of respondents' contacts with neighbors
and friends. They asked about the number of really good friends
who lived within an hour's drive, the length of time respondents
had lived in their present neighborhood, and their memberships
in voluntary associations. The researchers then looked at the
relationship between economic hardship, social isolation, and
depression. The unmarried, they found, were doubly burdened.
The unmarried were more likely to experience economic strain
and social isolation. Furthermore, the same levels of strain and
isolation were more strongly associated with depression among
the unmarried than the married. This finding was equally true for
blacks and whites and for the young and old. The married appeared to be doubly protected. They were less likely to experience
economic hardship and social isolation, but when they did, marriage seemed to provide some level of protection. The same was
true for parenting. Unmarried parents were considerably more
susceptible to depression than were married parents, especially
when family responsibilities were most demanding, that is, when
there were three or more children and when the children were
young. Pearlin and Johnson's (1977) findings, then, supported the
notion that marriage is beneficial to well-being. Marriage, it
seems, provides protective benefits above and beyond those that
emanate from reductions in economic hardship and social isolation. The source of the additional benefit, however, remained
unknown.

❧ Gender Differences in Well-Being Among the Married: Alternative Explanations

Whereas Pearlin and Johnson questioned the extent to which
marriage is really beneficial, others questioned the extent to which
it is marriage that best explains the well-being deficits in married

women compared to married men. At least three alternative explanations have been posed. These include gender differences in help-seeking behavior, sex-linked biological differences that make women more vulnerable to depression, and culturally learned differences in the characteristics that men and women seek in desirable marriage partners. Although research in each of these areas is neither as extensive nor definitive as one might wish, reviews of the literature conclude that none of the explanations fully explain the gender differences in well-being among the married (Nolen-Hoeksema, 1987, 1990; Weissman & Klerman, 1977).

Gender Differences in Help-Seeking Behavior

The first explanation for the discrepancy between husbands' and wives' well-being examines gender differences in help-seeking behavior and self-expression. Acknowledging the need for help (professional or otherwise) or that one is feeling badly is generally viewed as being less acceptable and therefore more costly for men than for women (Phillips & Segal, 1969). Consistent with this position, epidemiological studies show that women go to mental health professionals more often than do men. The question, then, is do women actually experience more distress or are they just more likely to report it and seek help? Conversely, are men actually equally distressed but just less likely to acknowledge it?

In the mid-'70s, a survey of help-seeking behavior was conducted on a representative sample of adults across the United States (Veroff, Kulka, Douvan, 1981). Women were more likely than men to use professional help for crises identified as interpersonal (divorce or relationship breakups). Men were more likely than women to seek help for problems defined as external (legal issues, money and job problems) and were also more likely than women to seek professional help for crises identified as "adjustment problems." Among those with less than a college education, women were more psychologically-minded than men and more likely to define a problem in mental health terms. Among the college educated, men were no less psychologically minded than women. For problems defined in mental-health terms, men, regardless of their education level, were no less likely than women to seek help.

A review of more recent studies found that men are just as likely to admit distress and seek help as women (Nolen-Hoeksema, 1987). Men were shown to be no less willing than women to disclose symptoms to researchers, and neither men nor women were less willing to disclose symptoms in public compared to private situations (Bryson & Pilon, 1984; King & Buchwald, 1982). In addition, and consistent with the earlier findings, studies of actual help-seeking behaviors found that men and women with similar levels of self-reported depressive symptoms were equally likely to seek psychiatric help or to go to a general practitioner (Amenson & Lewinsohn, 1981). Overall, then, the pattern of findings provides little support for the hypothesis that gender differences in well-being among the married are merely an artifact of gender differences in help-seeking behavior.

Sex Differences in Biological Vulnerability

Proponents of the biological position assert that it's not just that women are more willing to acknowledge distress but that they actually experience a greater number of problems. Epidemiological studies consistently show that women are twice as likely to be depressed as men. According to the biological position, however, this gender difference in the incidence of depression is better explained by biological vulnerability than by marriage. Two types of biological explanations have been posed. The first suggests that women are particularly prone to distress during times of significant hormonal changes. For adult women, these include menstruation, pregnancy, the postpartum period, and menopause. The second explanation suggests that women are more susceptible to depression because of a gene on the X chromosome. Because women have two X chromosomes (and men only one), it is argued that this leads to a higher risk of depression in women.

Reviews of the relevant research suggest that neither hormonal nor genetic explanations are well supported. Menopausal and long-term postpartum depression are rare, and evidence of significant premenstrual depression is found only in studies in which women are made aware of the focus of the study, suggesting an expectancy effect. Similarly, although there is evidence that affective disorders do run in families, support for the X chromosome hypothesis is both limited and inconsistent (Kelsoe et al., 1991). Although research in this area is still ongoing, the general conclusion is that although hormonal and genetic factors may play a role, biological explanations alone cannot fully account for gender differences in well-being among the married.

Gender Differences in Mate Selection

The final explanation focuses on gender differences in the characteristics that men and women seek in selecting desirable marriage partners. As originally noted by Bernard (1982), later studies consistently show that women and men tend to marry mates within their same general class and cultural background. Within that common background, however, women have been socialized to marry men they can "look up to" both literally and figuratively. Women seek to marry men who are taller, better educated, and whom they expect to be more successful than themselves. Men, in contrast, marry "down," that is, to women who are shorter, younger, and in less-lucrative and less-prestigious occupations. Because women tend to marry "up," it is hypothesized that those who never marry represent the "cream of the crop," that is, they are successful women for whom there is no man left to look up to. Because men, in contrast, are more likely to marry "down," those who never marry are more likely to represent men whom no woman *can* look up to. According to this hypothesis, these gender differences in marriage preferences explain why, among the never married, women often show less symptomatology than men, whereas among the married, men consistently show less symptomatology than women.

Many may wish to dismiss these notions as stereotypical and dated. Yet when contemporary college students were asked to define the characteristics they were looking for in their future partners, women gave greater importance to career success traits than did men (Gilbert, 1993). Other studies have shown that marital satisfaction can be linked to husbands' and wives' perceptions of husbands as superior (Yogev, 1987). Even women who achieve high levels of success in their careers are likely to believe that not only will their husbands achieve greater success than they will, but that their husbands are more intelligent than they are (Vannoy-Hiller & Philliber, 1989). Silberstein (1992), in a series of interviews with contemporary dual-career couples, concluded that the enduring expectation is for the man's career to be more important and for the man to earn more money and be more successful. Although wives' expectations of their partners' greater career success may reflect the realities of societal discrimination, subsequent chapters will show that this is not the whole story. Furthermore, it does not explain wives' beliefs in their husbands' superior intelligence.

Studies of personal ads in magazines and newspapers show that gender differences in age preferences also persist. Men who give their age in these ads want to hear from women who are from 9 years younger to 2 years older than themselves, whereas the reverse is true for women. Women want to hear from men who are from 2 years younger to 8 years older (Rajecki, Bledsoe, & Rasmussen, 1991). For men, those whose ads received the most responses were 11 years older than those who received the fewest responses. Again, the reverse was true for women. Those who received the most responses were 13 years younger than those who received the fewest responses. Women, it seems, still prefer men who are older, whereas men continue to prefer women who are younger. Why? Does age still hold connotative differences for men and women? With age, men have a better chance to demonstrate their career success characteristics and their capacity to be good protectors and providers. Conversely, cultural standards continue to define beauty partly in terms of youthful looks (Buss, 1994).[3] Are men, then, still "success objects" and women still "sex objects"? And are these gender differences in marriage preferences actually related to the well-being differences among the married?

The answer to the second question is a somewhat qualified no. There is little evidence to support the hypothesis that gender differences in marriage preferences have a direct effect on husbands' and wives' well-being. Yet the extent to which women continually seek to marry men who are older, bigger, stronger, smarter, more successful, and more accomplished than they

(Rubin, 1983), has clear implications for gender differences in marital power, the relationship of which to well-being is discussed in subsequent chapters.

✦ Additional Studies

Carmen, Russo, and Miller (1981) expanded Bernard's focus by examining the extent to which the "protective status" of marriage was consistent in reducing vulnerability to mental illness across race as well as gender. An index based on the proportional difference between the rates of illness among the married compared to the never married showed a 71% reduction in vulnerability to mental illness for minority-race men who married, a 63% reduction for white men, but only a 28% reduction for white women and a mere 8% reduction for minority-race women. Similarly, Bebbington (1987) found that marriage had less of a protective effect for women than men in England, and two additional studies found that marriage had little, if any, protective effect for women who were black (Taylor, Henderson, & Jackson, 1991; Waldron & Jacobs, 1989).

Gove (1973) looked at the relationship between sex, marital status, and mortality. He found that the married had lower mortality rates than the never married, widowed, or divorced, and that the differences between the married and the unmarried were greater for men than for women. According to Gove, these findings were true primarily for the types of mortality in which one's psychological state is most likely to affect one's life chances. These included death by suicide, homicide, and accident; alcoholism; and diseases, such as tuberculosis, that require extended and careful treatment regimens.

To pick an extreme example, Gove found that the likelihood of being murdered decreased for men when they were married. However, the reverse was true for women. For women, the shift from being single to being married increased the likelihood of being murdered. Although this example may seem particularly macabre, the fact is that more than half of all women murdered in the United States during the first half of the 1980s (52%) were victims of partner homicide (Browne & Williams, 1989).

◖ Qualifications and Caveats

In the years since the publication of Bernard's book, the findings and the hypotheses have been continually revisited. Although there is consistent evidence of support, some studies have only partially replicated the original findings, whereas others have suggested qualifications to consider. D'Arcy and Siddique (1985) re-examined Bernard's hypotheses using three large sets of data from Canada. Consistent with Bernard, they found that married men reported significantly lower levels of distress than married women and concluded that marriage does not give women the same benefits in reducing mental illness that it gives to men. Similarly, Fox (1980) also examined data from three large community surveys. As had Bernard (1982) and Gove (1972), Fox found that among the married, women had higher symptomatology than men. Unlike Bernard, Fox did not find that never-married women fared better than never-married men. In two of the three samples, there were no gender differences in well-being among the unmarried. In the third sample, Fox found that unmarried women reported more psychological symptomatology than unmarried men.

Still other scholars have suggested that Bernard's findings may be somewhat biased as a result of the kinds of symptoms and disorders that were studied (Bachrach, 1975; Dohrenwend & Dohrenwend, 1976). Although all agree that women are almost twice as likely to become depressed as are men, men may be more likely to be hospitalized for other kinds of problems that were not considered. Russo (1990) and Hankin (1990), in more recent reviews, concluded that women clearly predominate in diagnoses of major depressive episodes, agoraphobia, and simple phobia. These were the kinds of illnesses that Bernard examined. Men, however, predominate in diagnoses that Bernard omitted, such as antisocial personality and alcohol abuse.

❧ Conclusions

So what can we conclude? Clearly, the relationships between sex, ethnicity, gender roles, and mental health are complex, and the findings are less than conclusive. Most researchers agree, however, that men and women tend to differ in the types of disorders they experience. Most also agree that marriage provides something of a protective function, but that the benefits of that protective function are unequally distributed. The extent of the unequal distribution is unclear, yet the majority of studies suggest that men disproportionately benefit from marriage. The reasons for the unequal distribution of benefits are also unclear. Bernard seemed to focus primarily on middle-class whites and the structural strains that the institution of marriage imposed on wives, particularly full-time housewives.

Today the demographics have changed and the majority of wives are no longer full-time homemakers. Indeed, as we shall see in Chapter 6, what was once viewed as "traditional," a fully employed husband, a full-time housewife, and two children, no longer represents the typical family situation. The focus of research has also changed. Investigators are less interested in whether or not marriage per se is less beneficial for women than in attempting to understand the ways in which specific aspects of marriage facilitate or impede well-being. There is a growing consensus that what is needed is a better understanding of the ways in which psychological, social, and cultural forces, including our conceptions of marriage and gender, contribute to the different patterns of well-being for men and women, particularly husbands and wives. To these issues we now turn and, as we shall see, Bernard's basic idea of a "his" and "her" marriage is still alive and well in the '90s.

❧ Notes

1. Bernard published the first edition of her book in 1972. Her findings were based on a secondary analysis of data collected by a number of other investigators primarily in the 1960s.

2. Most of the post-Bernard studies reported here and throughout the book examine psychological symptomatology rather than subjective well-being. Campbell, Converse, and Rogers (1976) compared one of the primary measures of subjective well-being, self-reported happiness, with other well-being measures. They concluded that the "happiness" questions primarily reflect one's immediate affective state. In addition, self-report measures of well-being are vulnerable to particular types of bias, such as social desirability. How socially acceptable, for example, is it to say that your marriage is *not at all happy*? And if you are willing to admit to yourself and to others that your marriage is only *somewhat* or *not at all* happy, don't you then incur the expectation that you should do something about it? And what if you think you can't do anything about it or are unwilling to do something about it? Concerns such as these may contribute to the finding that the vast majority of respondents describe their marriages as *very happy*.

Studies of psychological symptomatology also use self-report measures, though less exclusively. Some studies use clinical interviews with trained professionals. Others use archival records, such as admissions to psychiatric hospitals. On the self-report measures, respondents are asked to tell how frequently in the last 2 weeks they've been bothered by specific types of symptoms such as loss of appetite, feeling blue, or having no energy. These types of questions may be somewhat less vulnerable to the biases of self-report than assessments of "happiness."

For those who are interested in the findings on subjective well-being, D'Arcy and Siddique (1985) found that married people of both sexes reported significantly higher personal happiness than never-married and formerly married people. Married men did not, however, report significantly greater happiness than married women (see also Campbell et al., 1976, and Glenn, 1975).

A meta-analysis conducted on 58 studies, each designed to assess the relationship between being married and subjective well-being, found that those who were married had higher levels of subjective well-being than those who were not married and that marriage was more strongly associated with well-being for men than for women, for younger-age compared to older-age samples, and in earlier research compared to more recent studies (Haring-Hidore, Stock, Okun, & Witter, 1985). Subjective well-being was defined to include studies of self-reported satisfaction with one's life, perceived quality of life, overall morale, and happiness. The meta-analysis did not compare differential effects for race or ethnicity. For a review of the literature on the relationship between marital status and sex differences in positive subjective well-being, see Wood, Rhodes, and Whelen, 1989.

3. Buss (1994) cites considerable evidence showing that men are more likely than women to seek youth and physical attractiveness in a mate, whereas women are more likely than men to seek status and economic security. Buss interprets these findings from an evolutionary perspective. For men, a woman's youth and physical attractiveness signal her reproductive value. For women, men's access to resources, earning power, and status increase the likelihood of having children who will "survive and thrive" (p. 7).

An alternative explanation, more consistent with the thesis of this book, interprets the gender differences in mate preferences from a sociostructural or power perspective. Women seek men who have power, status, and earning power because, traditionally, the social structure has disproportionately limited women's independent access to these resources. Men seek physical beauty in a mate to further enhance their own status. As Buss (1994) notes, " 'trophy' wives are not just the perquisites of high status, but in fact increase the status of men who can win them" (p. 59).

2

Social Roles and Psychological Well-Being

Paid Employment Versus Full-Time Homemaking

Our usual social institutions (including, among others, marriage, family relations, and child-rearing) have a differential and more stressful impact on women.

Report of the Special Populations Subpanel of the President's Commission on Mental Health, 1978, p. 1

❧ Investigations of the Social Roles Hypothesis

As noted in the first chapter, Bernard (1972) asserted that the gender differences in well-being among the married are attributable to differences in women's and men's social roles. She, and others, focused on the psychological costs of "housewifery"[1] and the lack of outside sources of gratification for unemployed women. Other scholars (Barnett, 1987; Oakley, 1974) have pointed out that housewifery usually involves multiple roles (mother, wife, and homemaker), all of which are assumed to fit easily together and none of which is viewed as a real "job." Yet the tasks associated with nurturing a child and those associated with keeping an attractive home are often highly incompatible (Oakley, 1974). In a series of in-depth interviews, Oakley asked 40 London housewives to list the best and worst aspects of being a housewife. The best aspects were listed as autonomy (i.e., the freedom to make one's own schedule) and children. The worst aspect, according to the respondents, was housework, described by the overwhelming majority as monotonous and boring, socially isolating and lonely, repetitive and never-ending, and universally devalued and trivialized, as exemplified in the phrase "just a housewife." The predominant feeling of Oakley's white middle-class and working-class respondents was one of profound dissatisfaction with housework.

Twenty years later, Oakley's findings held true for full-time houseworkers in the United States Houseworkers reported more routinization, less recognition, but more autonomy than paid workers. Over 88% of those doing full-time unpaid domestic work in a national probability sample were women. Men and women alike, however, reported housework to be less fulfilling and to provide less recognition than paid work, volunteer work, school work, or home and yard maintenance (Bird & Ross, 1993).

During the late '70s and early '80s, several studies were conducted to assess the extent to which well-being differences among the married could be explained by the social roles hypothesis (Aneshensel, Frerichs, & Clark, 1981; Cleary & Mechanic, 1983; Gore & Mangione, 1983; Gove & Geerken, 1977; Radloff, 1975). Employed husbands (with and without children), employed wives (with and without children), and full-time homemaker wives (with and without children) were compared on a number of measures of well-being, including feelings of loneliness, anxiety, and depression. Across all of these studies, employed husbands consistently fared best. Employed husbands showed the lowest levels of symptomatology, whether or not their wives were employed and whether or not they had children.[2] The studies also showed that employed wives never fared worse, and often fared better, than full-time homemaker wives. Unemployed homemakers often reported the highest prevalence of psychiatric symptoms and experienced the highest incidence of depression. Echoing Oakley's sample of London women, full-time homemakers, more than employed husbands or wives, reported that they felt confronted by incessant demands, that they more frequently desired to be alone, and that they more frequently felt lonely (Gove & Geerken, 1977).

Other findings, specifially those relating to the benefits of wives' employment, are more complex. In some studies, employed wives experienced less distress than housewives, but the presence of young children in the household was especially stressful. This was true for middle-class and working-class wives but sometimes especially the case for those with the lowest family incomes (Aneshensel et al., 1981; Cleary & Mechanic, 1983). In other studies, employed wives fared better than unemployed wives only when happiness with their jobs and their marriages was held constant. Thus, among women who were equally happy with their marriages, those who were employed and happy with their jobs fared better than those who were not employed (Radloff, 1975).

The findings relative to parental status are particularly complex. Fatherhood seems to have no negative effects on husbands' well-being. Indeed, some studies show employed married fathers experiencing higher well-being than any other group (Gore & Mangione, 1983).[3] In contrast, however, parenthood is often related to poorer well-being for mothers. In some studies, paid employment seems to provide a buffering effect for mothers, such that those who were employed showed fewer negative symptoms than did full-time housewives (Gore & Mangione, 1983). In other studies, however, stresses associated with the presence of young children at home seemed to undermine the benefits of employment, such that mothers who were employed fared no better than those who were home full-time (Aneshensel et al., 1981).

What, then, can we conclude? The findings relative to employed husbands are clear. Across all studies, husbands consistently showed the lowest levels of symptomatology. The findings relative to wives, however, are less straightforward. Although employed wives never fared worse than full-time housewives, they sometimes fared better when happiness with their jobs, their marriages, and their children were taken into consideration. This was not the case for husbands. Indeed, married employed husbands who were parents often reported the lowest symptomatology levels of all.

Full-time housewives often fared worse than employed wives, but the findings did not identify the detrimental characteristics of housewifery. In addition, the studies offered no explanation for why employed wives never fared as well as employed husbands. How can we explain these differences? Are the well-being differences between employed men and employed women explained by the differences in men's and women's jobs? By women's role overload? Or role conflict? Are the differences in well-being better explained by some yet-to-be-defined aspect of the marital relationship? Or by some combination of all these factors?

The Costs of Women's Paid Employment: Assumptions Versus Empirical Evidence

During the '70s and '80s, as women increasingly moved into the labor force, a number of questions were raised regarding the effect of women's employment on their own and their families' well-being. There seemed to be a general assumption that the world of paid employment would be experienced by women as harsher and more stressful than that of the home. Few questioned the additional assumption that women would simply add the responsibilities of paid employment to those of the home, and this gave rise to concerns of role overload (having to do too much) and role conflict (that fulfilling the demands of one role—e.g., paid employment—would interfere or preclude the ability to fulfill the demands of other roles—e.g., homemaking). As a result, the primary expectation was that labor-force participation would be detrimental to women and their children.

Contrary to expectation, however, there is no evidence of any negative effects of paid employment, per se, on women (Repetti, Matthews, & Waldron, 1989; Warr & Parry, 1982). Across both race (Guarnaccia, Angel, & Worobey, 1991; Ross, Mirowsky, & Ulbrich,

1983) and class (Ferree, 1976; Scarr, Phillips, & McCartney, 1989), the role of paid worker seems to be a source of independent identity, increased self-esteem, purposefulness, enhanced social contacts, and inherent interest (Barnett & Baruch, 1985; Coleman, Antonucci, Adelmann, & Crohan, 1987; Thoits, 1986; Weissman & Paykel, 1974). According to Barnett and Baruch (1985), the role of paid worker is less stressful to women than their more traditional roles and, of those, being a mother may be the most important source of stress in women's lives. Motherhood's unique combination of relentless demands, great responsibility, and minimal control are cited as factors in the finding that motherhood is rarely associated with improvements in well-being for women and is often associated with distress.

Yet mothers' employment seems to have no negative effects on their children. Reviews of all the studies to date indicate that children of employed mothers perform no worse on measures of school achievement, IQ test scores, or emotional and social development than children of unemployed mothers (Hoffman, 1987; Scarr et al., 1989). Indeed, daughters of employed mothers are often reported to be more independent, more self-confident, and more likely to achieve better grades than daughters of full-time housewives. In addition, it appears that sons and daughters of employed mothers hold more egalitarian sex-role attitudes and view women (and their own mothers) as more competent (Spitze, 1988).

Differences in the Benefits of Women's Paid Employment: Individual, Occupational, and Relationship Factors

Although the evidence suggests that there are no negative effects of paid employment on women or their children, the benefits are not the same for all women and are generally less than the benefits that accrue to men. For women, the benefits are influenced by a number of individual, occupational, and relationship factors. Mothers working in companies offering flexible work schedules experience less depression than mothers employed by companies without flexible schedules (Barling & Barenbrug, 1984). Though being employed has been shown to be beneficial to women regardless of job status, women in higher-status jobs enjoy more well-being benefits than women in lower-status jobs (Belle, 1982). Women in higher-status jobs often hold positions characterized by greater control, autonomy, interest, challenge, and flexibility (Puglieski, 1988); have more resources for better child care; and are more likely to emphasize the centrality of paid employment in their lives (Burris, 1991). In a recent study underscoring both the importance of paid employment and the conditions of that employment, 87% of 300 career women ages 35 to 49 said that they had made or were seriously considering major changes. Contrary to expectation, however, these women were neither intending to stop paid employment nor to go home to have or take care of children. Rather, the vast majority of these managerial women were seeking to find or create alternatives that allowed them greater flexibility and self-determination (Morris, 1995). These women, then, did not want to relinquish their careers. What they sought was to modify them.

Blue-collar women have fewer options than their white-collar counterparts, are more likely to work because of economic necessity, and traditionally have contributed proportionately more to the family income. Yet after reviewing the literature, Warr and Parry (1982) concluded that there was a stronger association between paid employment and improved well-being for working-class women than for their middle-class counterparts. Furthermore, surveys of working-class and black mothers showed they are quite committed to their jobs (Scarr et al., 1989), and the majority of these women said they would work even if they didn't need the money (Ferree, 1976; Malson, 1983). Indeed, despite the importance of their earnings, studies of both black and white working-class job applicants found that they ranked intrinsic rewards, such as the chance to learn new things and the chance to use skills and abilities, as more important than pay (Harris & Earle, 1986). A survey of 3,000 working mothers conducted in 1990 found that 92% of the respondents said they achieved a sense of well-being from their financial contributions to the family welfare, 80% said their jobs made them more interesting, more than three fourths said that their jobs boosted their self-esteem and that their children were more independent as a result of their working outside the home, and more than half said they wouldn't quit their jobs even if they could afford to do so.

On the individual level, psychological well-being is mediated by a number of attitudes and beliefs. Among women who are employed, those who perceive paid employment to be desirable are less depressed and less anxious than women who are employed but prefer to be home full-time. There is a parallel effect for husbands. Wives' employment is infrequently negatively associated with husbands' well-being (Burke & Weir, 1976) but, when it is, it is only for husbands who believe their wives should be home full-time (Kessler & McRae, 1982). Furthermore, husbands who oppose their wives' employment are more depressed if their own earnings are low than if their earnings are high (Ulbrich, 1988). Taken together, these findings suggest it is not wives' employment per se that is associated with decrements in well-being for men. Rather, the source of the distress may lie in a husband's belief that his wife's employment is inconsistent with what "should" be and somehow reflects negatively on him. Among employed mothers, those who endorse conservative gender-role ideologies (Parry, 1987) and those who believe that maternal employment has negative effects on children are more likely to be depressed than those who endorse more liberal ideologies and who see maternal employment as either benign or beneficial (Steil, Smrz, Wilkens, & Barnett, 1995).

The benefits of paid employment for women are also influenced by a number of relationship factors. Women whose husbands support their employment both behaviorally, by sharing the responsibilities of the home and children, and attitudinally, by respecting the importance of their wives' work, are less depressed than women who have unsupportive husbands (Amaro, Russo, & Johnson, 1987; Elman & Gilbert, 1984; Hughes & Galinsky, 1994; Kessler & McRae, 1982; Krause & Markides, 1985; Ross, Mirowsky, & Huber, 1983; Ulbrich, 1988). Similarly, women who are able to find reliable, quality child care (Ross & Mirowsky, 1988) are less depressed than women who have unsatisfactory child care (Hughes & Galinsky, 1994). Thus, independent of race and class, the quality of a woman's work life is linked not only to characteristics of her work environment but also to the quality of her parental and marital relationships (Baruch, Biener, & Barnett, 1987; Kessler & McRae, 1982).

Yet women receive less emotional and instrumental support from their spouses than do men. Husbands receive more emotional support than their wives (a topic to which we shall return in Chapter 5) and women, when they are employed, continue to do at least two thirds of the domestic work (a topic to which we shall return in Chapter 4). Women are also more affected by the presence of children and the availability of child care than are their husbands.

Why do employed wives receive less emotional and instrumental support than employed husbands? Why are employed mothers, more than employed fathers, affected by the availability of child care? Are these important factors in understanding the differences in well-being among employed husbands and wives? If so, how should they be construed? Should the differences in vulnerability to child care and the differences in spousal support be understood as just another aspect of the social roles hypothesis? Or do they reflect some other underlying dimension of marital relationships, such as differences in status or power? Or, we might ask, are differences in social roles and differences in marital power the same issue? And how do they relate to matters of well-being?

‰ Marital Power

Over a decade ago, in the course of reviewing the literature on families (Steil, 1983), I observed that the distribution of power between husbands and wives closely paralleled the patterns of well-being among the married. Power, at that time, was usually assessed as "say in decision making." Integrating what up until that time had been relatively discrete bodies of literature (that on family power and that on well-being), it seemed that employed husbands had the greatest decision-making say in their marriages and scored highest on measures of well-being. Unemployed housewives had the least decision-making say in their marriages and scored lowest on measures of well-being, and employed wives scored somewhere in between employed husbands and unemployed wives on both decision making and well-being (Steil, 1983, 1984).

Returning, then, to Bernard's middle-class housewives, an examination of the factors associated with marital power suggested that these women were likely to have less power in their relationships than almost any other group. Black wives are believed to have more marital power than white wives, and black couples seem to be more egalitarian about gender roles than white couples (Beckett & Smith, 1981; Ericksen, Yancey, & Ericksen, 1979; Scanzoni & Szinovacz, 1980), a topic that will be revisited in Chapter 4. Employed wives have more say in marital decisions than wives who are unemployed; and among employed wives, number of years worked, continuity, and pattern of employment (Weingarten, 1978), such as whether employment was initiated before or after marriage (Ray, 1990), are all associated with increases in a wife's influence. Employed wives are less likely than housewives to endorse traditional sex-role ideologies (Dugger, 1988; Mason & Bumpass, 1975; Mason, Czajka, & Arber, 1976) and are more likely to have smaller families (Spitze, 1988). Family size is also associated with marital power, such that wives with no or few young children have greater influence than those with more children. Among housewives, the higher a husband's income, the more likely his wife is to endorse the legitimacy of his power (Scanzoni, 1972).

A wife's influence seems to be greatest, then, when there are no or few young children, when the gap between her own and her husband's income is proportionately small, and when she continuously pursues a full-time career that was initiated before her marriage. Women under these conditions also seemed to experience the highest levels of physical and psychological well-being. Integrating this varied collection of findings, I hypothesized that differences in spousal support and in husbands' and wives' well-being might best be construed as a reflection of the differences in husbands' and wives' marital power. A few years later, I tested that hypothesis.

❧ Notes

1. During the 1970s, the term *housewife* was commonly used. Today the literature more commonly uses the terms *homemaker* or *houseworker*. In keeping with the literature of that time, however, I have sometimes retained the authors' use of *housewife*.

2. Unemployed husbands were not represented in many of these studies. It is well established, however, that unemployment is associated with reductions in influence and poor psychological well-being for husbands. Thus, it is a reflection of the pervasiveness and power of the ideology of separate gender roles that the underlying assumption of much of this research was that paid employment was unquestionably beneficial to men but most likely harmful to women.

3. This may not be the case for black fathers. Taylor, Chatters, Tucker, and Lewis (1990) note in a review of research on black families that "although the diverse effects of parental status on psychological well-being have been routinely investigated among whites, these issues remain a neglected area of research among blacks" (p. 1000). As well, Browman (1991) notes that the significance of marital and parental status to the psychological well-being of blacks is poorly understood. In 1991, Browman found that nonemployed men who were parents had higher levels of life satisfaction than men who were employed parents. In 1993, he found that black men with children living in the home reported lower levels of marital harmony than white men or women or black women. This was the case even when age, education, family income, and employment status were considered. Clark-Nicolas and Gray-Little (1991) found that having more children was associated with lower levels of marital satisfaction among low-income black men but not among black men with higher incomes.

3

The Relationship
Between Marital Power
and Partners' Well-Being

Marriage has been many things, but at all times it has been a relationship of power, however muted or disguised it may be in any particular case.

Degler, 1980, p. 29

Marriage has a differential and more stressful impact on women than on men because of the inequality in the status of husbands and wives.

Report of the Special Populations Subpanel of the President's Commission on Mental Health, 1978, p. 1

In 1978, the President's Commission on Mental Health concluded that marriage was more stressful for women than for men because of the difference in status ascribed to the gendered work of husbands and wives. Although the previous chapters have emphasized some of the undesirable qualities of wives' homemaking work, (i.e., lack of structure, repetitiveness, and social isolation), the report of the President's Commission focused less on the characteristics of the work itself than on the ways in which wives' work is perceived and valued differently from husbands' work.

History shows us that work has often been divided along gender lines, but it is only in recent times that the work of the home has become so physically and emotionally separate from work outside the home. During the colonial period, for example, the family functioned as a business, a school, a training institution, and a church. In Plymouth colony, women, with the help of their children, assumed the bulk of internal domestic chores. They took care of the house, including the preparation of food, cloth, candles, and soap. They supervised the farm animals and kitchen garden while husbands did the plowing, planting, and harvesting (Bernard, 1981; Kessler-Harris, 1982). Yet "interaction never stopped. Husbands helped with spinning and weaving when farm work was done. Mothers taught young children their letters . . . fathers tended to take over the educational process as (children) grew older" (Kessler-Harris, 1982, p. 7). In the southern colonies, male apprentices often did household chores. Wives routinely developed competence in their husbands' business.

As is the case today, "domestic work fell low on any hierarchical scale" and the role of wife was secondary to the role of husband (Kessler-Harris, 1982, p. 7). Yet unlike today, "the idea [was] seldom encountered that a man supports his wife; [rather] husband and wife were mutually dependent and together supported the children" (p. 7).[1]

By the end of the 18th century, manufactured products began to replace those formerly made in the household. As the country moved toward a market economy, both men and women began to enter the paid labor force; but as industrialization accelerated, waged work was increasingly viewed as improper for women. Black and immigrant women took low-paying domestic and factory work, but among the middle and upper classes, women stayed home while men left to enter the worlds of business and industry.

Dichotomization gave birth to ideology. Because men were removed from contact with children, women assumed greater responsibility for the training and supervision of their offspring. "Motherhood rose to new heights and children became the focus of womanly activity" (Kessler-Harris, 1982, p. 50). At the same time, "men who worked hard to achieve success in the wider world needed wives who were emotionally supportive and who could manage the household competently" (p. 50). For the urban middle class, "womanhood came to serve as the repository of the higher moral and ethical values lost in the cold business community" (p. 50). Among the less affluent, home came to be viewed as a sanctuary and a retreat. Simultaneous with these changes, being a good husband came to mean being a good provider, and being a good wife came to mean being a good homemaker and mother (Bernard, 1981; Degler, 1980).

Although both providing and homemaking can be seen as valued expressions of family responsibility and caring, dichotomization of these roles led to further devaluation. Husbands' provider role was associated with higher status and greater power than wives' housekeeping and nurturing roles. Indeed, as the value and significance of domestic work was undermined, the work of the home came to be viewed less in terms of shared responsibility and caring and increasingly as low-status work performed by the less-powerful partner.

The emphasis of the commission's report, then, was not so much on the nature or the amount of work that women do but on how *what* they do reflects an inequality of status. Furthermore, it found that the inequality of power and status, rather than marriage per se, causes the differential well-being of husbands and wives.

Power has been defined as the ability to influence important decisions (Blumstein & Schwartz, 1983) and to get others to do what they otherwise wouldn't. Because studies consistently show that husbands are unwilling to assume responsibility for domestic work, the extent to which they do assume such responsibilities has been viewed as a measure of the relative power of the partners. At the time of the commission's report, a number of studies showed that husbands generally had more say in decision making and did less domestic work than wives, even when their wives were employed. Studies also showed that husbands experienced greater well-being compared to wives. Indeed, as we saw in Chapter 2, research showed that employed husbands had the greatest decision-making say in their marriages and scored highest on measures of well-being. Unemployed housewives had the least decision-making say in their marriages and scored lowest on measures of well-being. Employed wives scored somewhere between on both. The fact that the patterns of marital power closely paralleled the patterns of well-being suggested a relationship between the two. Yet few, if any, studies directly assessed the relationship between the way that marital power was shared and partners' well-being. The findings of the commission's report, then, rested on inference rather than explicit evidence.

By the mid-'80s, however, the picture was beginning to change. A number of investigators began to explore the hypothesis that the gender differences in well-being among the married might be explained by gender differences in marital power. In 1987, Beth Turetsky and I undertook an empirical test of that hypothesis using a sample of 815 dual-career couples (Steil & Turetsky, 1987a, 1987b).

❧ The Relationship Between Marital Power and Partners' Well-Being: An Empirical Test

Sample Characteristics

We tested the relationship between marital power and psychological well-being using data from a sample of 815 primarily white dual-career couples who had participated in a national survey on paid employment and family work (Zeitz, 1981). Full-time housewives were not represented because we were trying to explain the gender differences in well-being among the employed. Because full-time housewives, as noted in the last chapter, generally have the least power in their relationships, we were trying to assess the extent to which differences in marital power explain the gender differences in well-being among a group of couples who would be expected to have the most equal relationships. Indeed, in comparison to national norms, the sample on which this study was conducted was younger, more highly educated, and more highly paid than average two-paycheck couples. Husbands, on average, were 2 years older than wives (33 vs. 31 years) and had worked two years longer (9.5 vs. 7.3 years). Forty percent of the sample had children, and over 40% were college graduates (44% of wives vs. 41% of husbands).

Say in Decision Making and
Responsibility Sharing

Consistent with previous studies, marital power was assessed by asking respondents to indicate, on a series of 5-point Likert scales, how the responsibility for making major decisions and the performance of a number of household and child-care tasks were allocated. Overall, and consistent with what we might expect for this sample, both husbands and wives reported that the sharing of responsibility was relatively equal in all areas.[2] Yet within this context of relative equality, spouses agreed that wives had more responsibility than husbands for household tasks and child care, whereas husbands had more responsibility for decision making. Although spouses agreed about who does more, they disagreed about how much more. Thus, although husbands and wives both agreed that wives had more responsibility for the children and the home, wives thought they did more than their husbands said they did, and husbands thought they did more than their wives gave them credit for.

Given the literature mentioned in the preceding chapter, which suggested that women who have children have the least influence in their relationships, we next divided the sample into four groups: employed husbands without children, employed wives without children, employed mothers, and employed fathers. As predicted in the literature (given the absence of full-time housewives in the sample), employed mothers seemed to have the least equal relationships. Among those with children, both husbands and wives agreed that wives had more responsibility than did husbands for child care and for the home. Furthermore, women who were mothers had less say in decision making than women who were not mothers. Because wives already had slightly less say than husbands, this finding suggested a further decline in influence for women when they became mothers.

Respondents were also asked how important they thought their own careers were relative to their spouses' careers. There were no differences between mothers and nonmothers in their ratings of the importance of their careers, but wives, overall, rated their husbands' careers as somewhat more important than their own.

Predictors of Decision-Making Say and Domestic Task Sharing

We next wanted to know what determines the amount of say that husbands and wives have and what determines how the responsibility for housekeeping and child care is allocated. A number of theorists believe that wives have less influence and do more work at home because they provide fewer outside resources to the family (Blood & Wolfe, 1960; Scanzoni, 1972). *Resources* have been defined as anything one partner brings to a relationship that helps the other partner satisfy needs or achieve goals. Yet economic resources, such as income and job prestige, seem to play a disproportionate role in determining marital influence (Kidder, Fagan, & Cohn, 1981). Husbands, who have traditionally earned more and held more prestigious jobs than wives, have had more financial and status resources to bring to the relationship and, according to some, these have been exchanged for greater authority and less work at home (Scanzoni, 1979). To test this idea, we looked at the effect of husbands' and wives' absolute earnings, their earnings relative to their spouses' earnings, and age, education, and perceived job importance as predictors of decision-making say and responsibility sharing.

Analyses showed no effect for partners' absolute earnings. Thus, how much one earned was unrelated to the amount of influence one had. One's earnings relative to one's spouse was an important predictor of marital power for women without children but was unrelated to the power of mothers. The more a woman without children earned relative to her husband, the less responsibility she had for the house and the greater her say in marital decisions. For women who were mothers, however, earnings relative to their spouses' earnings were unrelated to any of the responsibility or influence variables. Thus, it seemed that earning power relative to one's spouse did not work the same way for women with children as it did for women without children.

When we looked at the effects of all the factors, we found that the single most important predictor overall was not any of the income variables but rather perceived career importance. For husbands and wives without children, the more important they perceived their own jobs to be, relative to their spouses' jobs, the more responsibility they had for decision making. Also, for mothers, the more they valued their own jobs relative to their husbands' jobs, the greater their say in decision making and the less responsibility they had for household tasks.

But child care was a different story. Neither perceived job importance nor earnings relative to her spouse were related to a mother's responsibility for child care. Thus, for mothers, no matter how much they earned, either in absolute terms or in relation to their spouses' earnings, and no matter how important they perceived their own job to be relative to their husbands' job, they still retained the major responsibility for the children.

Well-Being

We wanted to look next at the relationship between decision-making say, responsibility sharing, and well-being. To assess well-being, husbands and wives were asked to report the extent to which they were bothered by 26 symptoms associated with either dysphoric (e.g., feeling worthless, lonely, sad, irritable, having trouble concentrating, or being bothered by irrational fears) or somatic (e.g., headaches, chest pains, upset stomach, or digestive problems) symptomatology (Derogatis, Lipman, Rickels, Uhlenhuth, & Coti, 1974; see Table 3.1).

Spouses' levels of somatic symptoms did not differ, and there were no differences on either of the symptom measures between those who had children and those who did not. Consistent with

Table 3.1   Items Comprising the Dysphoric and Somatic Symptomatology Scales[a]

Dysphoria	*Somaticism*
Constant worry/anxiety	Headaches
Tiring easily	Digestive problems
Feeling I just can't go on	Stomach ulcers or colitis
Crying easily	Chest pains
Feeling lonely	Nausea, upset stomach
Lack of interest in or pleasure in sex	Recurring diarrhea
Feeling irritable or angry	Chronic constipation
Feeling sad or depressed	Trouble getting my breath
Feeling shy or self-conscious	
Trouble concentrating	
Feeling tense or keyed up	
Irrational fears	

a. These scales were created using factor analysis. Three items (poor appetite, insomnia, and feeling fat) did not fall clearly on either factor and were therefore deleted.

the literature mentioned in the previous chapters, however, wives reported more dysphoria than did husbands.

Marital Satisfaction, Career Satisfaction, and Psychological Well-Being

Before we tested the hypothesis about whether or not the amount of power or say a partner had was related to the amount of psychological distress he or she reported, we had to consider what other factors, such as job and career satisfaction, might also be important. Overall, the respondents in this sample indicated that they were highly satisfied with their marriages and fairly satisfied with their careers. Wives were somewhat more satisfied with their careers than were husbands, and mothers were somewhat less satisfied with their marriages than were women without children. Consistent with the literature mentioned in Chapter 2, this was not the case for fathers. Fathers were no less satisfied with their marriages than nonfathers. When we looked at the relationship between career and marital satisfaction and psychological well-being, we found that for all four groups, the more satisfied they were with their careers and their marriages, the less dysphoria they reported.[3]

Domestic Task Sharing and Psychological Well-Being

We then turned to the primary question of the study: To what extent did say in decision making and responsibility for domestic work predict the frequency of husbands' and wives' self-reported symptoms after marital and career satisfaction were considered? For those with the most power, that is, husbands (with and without children) and wives without children, there was little relationship between the measures of marital influence and well-being. Indeed, the only relationship to reach significance was contrary to our hypotheses. For husbands without children, the more they shared in the work of the home, the *less* dysphoric symptomatology they reported (see Table 3.2).

When we considered the relationships between responsibility, influence, and well-being among those with the least influence, that is, the employed mothers, we found quite a different picture. Here, the relationships were quite strong (see Table 3.2). The more equal a mother's say in decision making and the more her husband shared in the responsibilities of child care, the less dysphoria she reported. She was less likely to report feeling lonely, sad, irritable, worried, tense, weepy, fearful, worthless, and disinterested in sex (see Table 3.1) . For mothers, then, greater husband involvement in child care and equal say in decision making were both associated with greater well-being. Contrary to expectation, however, increased husband responsibility for household tasks was associated with higher, rather than lower, levels of dysphoric symptoms for the mothers in this sample.

Why should greater husband involvement in household tasks be associated with greater distress for their partners? Because the relationships were correlational, we wondered if it were the case that husbands did the most work when wives were most dis-

Table 3.2 The Relationship Between Career Satisfaction, Marital Satisfaction, Marital Influence, and Dysphoric Symptomatology Levels for Husbands and Wives, With and Without Children[a]

	Variable	beta	R^2 Change	F	beta	R^2 Change	F
		Wives With Children			Husbands With Children		
Step 1	Career satisfaction	-.17	.04	7.44*	-.14	.02	5.53**
	Marital satisfaction	-.27	.11	19.96*	-.32	.13	28.17*
Step 2	Decision-making say squared[b]	.15	.02	5.39**	.03	.00	1.00
	Decision-making say	-.03	.00	.24	.01	.00	1.00
	Home responsibility	.22	.02	12.13*	-.08	.01	1.94
	Child responsibility	-.16	.05	6.26**	-.10	.01	2.96
		Wives Without Children			Husbands Without Children		
Step 1	Career satisfaction	-.25	.10	30.20*	-.28	.08	36.63*
	Marital satisfaction	-.27	.07	33.54*	-.29	.12	40.62*
Step 2	Decision-making say squared	.01	.00	.03	.06	.00	1.45
	Decision-making say	.05	.00	1.04	.05	.00	1.33
	Home responsibility	.01	.00	.10	-.10	.01	4.70**
	Child responsibility	—	—	—	—	—	—

a. Data were analyzed using hierarchical regression procedures. For the Satisfaction variables, the higher the score, the greater the respondent's satisfaction. For the responsibility variable, the higher the score, the greater responsibility (or decision-making say) the husband is perceived to have.

b. The decision-making say squared variable tests the extent to which both partners having equal say in decision making and predicts symptomatology levels. A similar variable could not be created for home or child responsibility because there were too few equally sharing couples.

*p<.01;
**p<.05.

tressed. Subsequent analysis, however, provided no support for this explanation. When we selected out the mothers who had symptomatology ratings at least one standard deviation above the mean, analysis showed that the husbands of the most distressed women assumed no more responsibility for household tasks than did other husbands in the sample.

Weiss (1987), among others, has shown that husbands do not modify their understandings of marital responsibilities when their wives are employed outside the home. Rather, they continue to believe that housekeeping is their wives' responsibility. Blumstein and Schwartz (1983) found that the more housework husbands did, the more couples fought about it. Do husbands who help resent it and extract a cost for their labors? Biernat and Wortman (1991) found that even when spouses each agreed to perform certain household chores, wives continued to assume responsibility for seeing that the chores got done. Was this, then, a cause of the stress?

Also possible is that women continue to feel that the home is their responsibility and that how it looks reflects more on them than on their husbands. Ferree (1991) found that two thirds of a representative sample of dual-earner wives said they tried to maintain the same standard of housework they would if they were not employed. One third of husbands, in this same sample, said that their housework contributions did not meet their wives' standards. What happens, then, when husbands have different standards for housework than their wives? Do wives have difficulty relinquishing control of the standards and is this, too, a partial cause of the fighting?

❧ Summary and Conclusions

What, then, do the findings of this study tell us? First of all, as noted earlier, this was a sample of dual-career couples in which unemployed housewives were unrepresented. Thus, we were asking whether differences in marital power (as measured by say in decision making and responsibility for domestic work) predict psychological symptomatology among a group of couples reporting relatively equal relationships. Yet within this overall context of relative equality, wives had somewhat less say in decision making and had somewhat more responsibility for the work of the home than had husbands. Wives with children bore the major responsibility for child care and had less say than their childless counterparts. Yet wives with children did not differ from wives without children in terms of symptom levels. Thus, it was not the presence of children, per se, that was associated with reductions in well-being. Rather, the arrival of children seemed to undermine the relative equality of the relationships by reactivating traditional gender roles, and it was this relative inequality that was associated with increases in psychological symptomatology. Thus, it was for the mothers, the "least equal" group, that unequal say in decision making and disproportionate responsibility for the children were most strongly associated with higher levels of psychological distress.

The findings, however, also raise a number of questions. Why do employed wives with children suffer a decline in influence compared to wives without children? Do they step back from their careers after the birth of their children and begin to de-emphasize the importance of their own jobs compared to their husbands'? There was no evidence of career de-emphasis on the part of the mothers in this sample. Mothers did not rate their careers as being less important. Furthermore, for this sample, the mothers actually reported somewhat higher earnings than their childless counterparts.[4]

Finally, the best predictor of the way that responsibility was shared was husbands' and wives' perceptions of the importance of their own careers relative to their spouses' careers. But what is perceived job importance really measuring? Is it measuring partners' self-esteem? Is it measuring their sense of entitlement to pursue their careers? Is it measuring a sense of entitlement to more equal sharing so that they *can* pursue their careers?

In addition to the questions raised, what do the findings of this study tell us? Consistent with the studies reported in the last chapter, the current findings again showed that the presence of children is associated with decreased marital power for mothers. They also showed that those with the least equal distribution of domestic responsibilities, the mothers, were the least satisfied with their marriages. And finally, the findings showed that marital satisfaction and the distribution of responsibilities are both related to the well-being of those with the least equal relationships. But how robust and how generalizable are these findings?

ᴥ Findings From Other Studies

During the 1980s, a number of investigators examined the relationship between decision-making say, involvement in domestic work, marital satisfaction, and partners' well-being. To what extent were the findings of these studies consistent with our own?

Decision Making and Marital Satisfaction

Gray-Little and Burks (1983) reviewed 12 studies assessing the relationship between say in decision making and marital satisfaction. Of the 12 studies, almost half were conducted in European countries, one was a study of Mexican American couples, and one a study of African American couples. The rest were studies of primarily white Americans conducted at sites across the United States. In 8 of the 12 studies, partners who reported that decision making was equally shared also showed the highest levels of marital satisfaction. Syncratic decision making, in which most decisions were made jointly, was associated with greater satisfaction than autonomic decision making, in which equal numbers of separate decisions were made by each partner. Husband dominance was linked with satisfaction in 2 of the 12 studies, including the one study of African Americans. For two of the studies, both conducted in Eastern Europe, the findings were inconclusive. Across all 12 studies, wife dominance was reported least often and was associated with the least satisfaction for men and women alike.

Lange and Worrell (1990) also surveyed the balance of power in relationships using a decision-making say measure. They found that husbands reported less satisfaction with their relationships when their wives had greater say than when say was equal or their own say was greater. Wives reported greater satisfaction when decision-making say was equally shared, compared to situations in which there was an imbalance on the part of either partner. In addition, husbands and wives who reported an equal balance of power gave and received higher levels of communal nurturance (i.e., positive regard, affirmation, and empathy) than those who were in relationships in which the power balance was unequal.

An observational study of decision making from the communication literature found that couples categorized as egalitarian by observers were more likely to use reason-giving in response to disagreement, to take the lead by giving opinions, give the lead by soliciting information, support the other's contributions, usually wait for the other's response before moving on, extend the other's comments, and build on the partner's previous statement (Krueger, 1975).

Some studies have examined the effect of unequal power on the dominant partner in dating and married couples. These studies showed that respondents who perceived themselves as controlling decision making rated themselves more favorably than they rated their partners, expressed less affection for their partner, were less attracted to, less satisfied, and less happy with the relationship, and had lower levels of sexual satisfaction (Kipnis, Castell, Gergen, & Mausch, 1976; Kipnis, Cohn, & Catalno, 1979). The effect of the unequal distribution of power on the less powerful partner was not investigated.

Domestic Task Sharing and Psychological Well-Being: Additional Studies

Several studies examined the relationship between partners' involvement in household labor and psychological well-being, specifically depressive or dysphoric symptoms (e.g., feeling blue, feeling worthless, tiring easily, or losing interest in sex). Three of these studies used large samples of married couples. All found some relationship between husbands' involvement in domestic responsibilities and wives' well-being.

Ross et al. (1983) found that husbands' help with household labor (a measure that included household tasks and child care and did not distinguish between the two) was associated with lower levels of depression in wives, whether or not the wife worked outside the home. Kessler and McRae (1982) found that employed wives whose husbands shared child care fared better on measures of self-esteem, dysphoria, and anxiety than did full-time home-makers or employed wives whose husbands did not share child care. Husbands' help with housework, however, was unrelated to wives' well-being. For husbands, neither involvement in child care nor housework was associated with well-being. Husbands who frequently did child care and housework were no more or less distressed than husbands who infrequently or never did either.

VanFossen (1981) studied the extent to which differences in partners' access to intimacy, affirmation and perceptions of reci-procity were associated with dysphoric symptomatology. Neither involvement in housework nor child care were assessed but rather the extent to which wives felt they "could rely" on their husbands for "help" with family problems. All wives, whether or not they were employed, were less depressed when they perceived their husbands to be "willingly helpful," compared to when they did not. Lack of affirmation (a negative endorsement of "my husband appreciates me just the way I am") was the best predictor of increased symptomatology for unemployed housewives. Lack of intimacy and affirmation were the best predictors of symptoma-tology levels for husbands. For employed wives, both lack of affirmation and perceptions of "inequity" (e.g., "my husband usually expects more from me than he is willing to give back") were the best predictors of symptomatology levels. Among em-ployed wives, the highest levels of dysphoric symptomatology were found among those who reported that they had too much to do, that they could not rely on their husbands for help, and that they and their husbands argued about who should do the work.

Each of these studies used large samples with varying income levels, but the respondents were usually exclusively or predomi-nantly white. Two other studies examined the relationship be-tween power and well-being in samples of Hispanic women. Kranau, Gree, and Valencia-Weber (1982) found that the more that husbands helped at home, the less mental distress Hispanic wives reported. Krause and Markides (1985) found that husbands' help with housework was more important than involvement in child care. They found no relationship between husbands' involvement in child care and wives' well-being, but employed wives who received very little or no help with housework showed higher levels of depressive symptoms than those who did receive help with housework.

Finally, Madden (1987) examined frequency of decision-making say, task performance, and perceived control over decision making and task performance among a sample of 37 working-class and professional couples. Findings showed that those who were most satisfied with their marriages reported that they and their partner shared task control equally.

ᴖ Summary of the Empirical Evidence

Overall, the general pattern of findings seems to support the notion that the ways in which domestic responsibilities and say in decision making are shared are related to partners' marital satisfaction and wives' psychological well-being. The findings of the studies of decision-making say are the most consistent and therefore easiest to interpret. These studies show that a wife's dominance in decision making, which is relatively rare, is associated with the lowest levels of marital satisfaction for both partners. A husband's dominance in decision-making say may be more frequently associated with satisfaction for husbands than for wives, whereas equal sharing may be associated with the highest levels of satisfaction for wives. When we consider other measures in addition to marital satisfaction, the findings suggest that relatively equal say is most beneficial for relationships. Relatively equal relationships were characterized by more mutually supportive communication, less manipulative forms of influence, and greater sexual and marital satisfaction for both partners than were relationships in which either one of the partners was dominant.

The findings of the studies of husband participation in domestic work are somewhat more difficult to interpret. In all of the studies, the responsibility for child care and housework was unequally distributed, with wives doing more than their husbands. In each of the studies, wives, whether or not they were employed, also reported higher symptomatology levels than their husbands. Yet whether the differences in well-being would have been eliminated if the relationships were equal could not be tested. There were too few equally sharing couples to study.

In addition, diverse measures were used in these studies. Some measures assessed perceptions of the way that responsibility was allocated, and some assessed the extent to which husbands "helped." But one partner "helping" the other is quite different from partners equally sharing responsibility. Still other measures assessed perceptions of "reciprocity." The assumption underlying all these studies was that say in decision making and allocation of domestic responsibilities are measures of marital power. Because child care and housework are generally viewed as low-status work, it is assumed that greater involvement in these tasks reflects less power in the relationship, whereas say in decision making reflects greater power in the relationship. Yet perceptions of power and status are never directly assessed.

With these important caveats, some of the patterns seem consistent. First of all, there is no evidence that husbands are impaired through increased participation in domestic work. Although it is true that husbands did less than wives, the fact that husbands' participation in housework did not cause reductions in well-being for men supports the notion that it is not just the nature of domestic work that impairs well-being. Because the studies compared employed wives and employed husbands, in addition to full-time homemakers, the findings suggest that it is not just the isolation and lack of alternative sources of gratification that cause impaired well-being. Rather, the fact that husbands' involvement in domestic work produced no measurable decrements in well-being seems to support the idea that the way that the work is viewed is more important than the nature of the work itself. Thus, the more a husband shares in the work of the home, the less it may seem that a person of lower status is doing menial work for a person of higher status, and the invidious message of a status difference is replaced by a sense of mutual cooperation and sharing.

There is also considerable evidence that husbands' increased participation is associated with less dysphoric symptomatology for wives. But the findings were not always consistent. Some studies showed reductions in symptomatology levels associated with husbands' increased participation in child care but not housework, some with increased participation in housework but not child care, and some for both. How can we explain this? First, and consistent with the opening comments in Chapter 2, it is clear that child care and housework are psychologically distinct. As the Steil and Turetsky (1987a, 1987b) study showed, earnings relative to one's spouse and one's perceived career importance predicted husbands' involvement in housework but not child care. Consistent with subsequent studies' findings, husbands' involvement in child care and domestic work were not associated in the same ways with wives' well-being. Once again, it seems that it is important to consider not only how much husbands and wives do but how what they do is perceived. None of these studies considered husbands' and wives' gender-role ideologies. But gendered beliefs, as we saw in Chapter 2, have been shown to be important determinants of perceptions. To what extent is a wife's identity defined by her role of homemaker and mother? To what extent is a husband's identity defined by his ability to provide? Do these gendered identities determine the ways in which men's domestic work is perceived—as willing participation in shared responsibilities? Or as threatening to husbands and wives alike? For some husbands, increased participation at home may challenge their masculine identity and their ability to meet career demands. For some wives, husbands' greater participation may threaten their view of themselves as adequate homemakers and mothers. To what extent, then, might individual differences in gender-role beliefs explain the inconsistencies in the findings?

The inconsistencies are exacerbated when we look at the limited number of studies among Hispanics. Yet there are no studies that systematically compare the relationship between partner well-being and partner involvement in child care and household work across ethnic groups and no studies of these relationships among blacks.

In short, the findings of the studies are consistent with the hypothesis that gender differences in emotional well-being and mental health are associated with gender differences in power and status. Yet they do not seem to tell the whole story, and they do not preclude other possible explanations. They do not examine the psychological meanings of housework, child care, or equal sharing for men or for women or across race and class. Thus, in some ways, they raise as many questions as they answer. Would the well-being differences be eliminated if relationships were in fact equal? Is it really equality of power that matters? Or is it something else? Partners' perceptions of their social roles? A sense of fairness? Perceptions of support? And if equality is important, how should it be defined? How should it be measured? Why does it matter? These, then, are some of the questions to which I will turn in subsequent chapters.

❧ Notes

1. Kessler-Harris takes this quote from Alice Clark (who used it in reference to 17th-century England) and applies it to the United States.

2. Means ranged from 2.69 to 3.18 on 5-point scales in which a 1 indicated that wives had almost all responsibility, a 5 indicated that husbands had almost all responsibility, and a 3 indicated that responsibility was equally shared.

3. For ease of presentation, I discuss only the findings for the measure of dysphoric symptomatology. The findings for somatic symptomatology followed a similar pattern; for a full report, see Steil & Turetsky, 1987a, 1987b.

4. Women with children were somewhat older than those without, perhaps explaining their higher earnings.

4

Relationship Equality

What Is It?
How Has It Been Measured?
Why Does It Matter?

Do you know any married couples who have a relationship that you think of as *equal*? What is it, specifically, about that couple's relationship that makes you think of it as equal?

Do you know any couples whose marriages you would consider to be *unequal*? What is it that makes you think of their relationship as unequal?

Rosenbluth, Steil, & Whitcomb, under revision

During the last two decades, social scientists of diverse orientations have begun to focus on the way that power is distributed and influence is exercised in intimate relationships. Some investigators have studied gender differences in influence strategy use. Others have focused on the extent to which power is equally shared. Of these, some have investigated the relationship benefits associated with equality, and others have focused on the psychological costs to the partners when relationships are unequal. In addition, a number of investigators have thought about these issues from the perspective of social justice theory, considering not only equality but also equity and need as principles on which intimate relationships might be based.

Within this varied literature, the concept of equality often remains undefined. Whereas equality in the workplace can be measured by explicit organizational criteria, defining equality in complex emotional relationships, in which needs and expectations are often implicit rather than explicit, has proved exceedingly difficult. How do social scientists think about and define equality in the context of an intimate relationship?

❧ Relationship Equality: The Social Scientists' Perspective

Peplau (1983), after studying a number of couple relationships, divided them into three types: traditional, modern, and egalitarian. The two dimensions on which these relationship types differ, according to Peplau, are (a) *power*, the extent to which the husband is more dominant than the wife, and (b) *role specialization*, the extent to which responsibilities are assigned on the basis of gender. According to Peplau, traditional marriages are based on a form of benevolent male dominance coupled with clearly specialized roles. Egalitarian marriages reject both of these ideas, and modern marriages represent a middle position. Gilbert (1985) also identifies three family types, which she calls traditional, participant, and role-sharing. In the *traditional* marriage, the responsibility for family work is retained by the woman, who adds the career role to her traditionally held family role. In the *participant* marriage, both partners are employed and parenting is shared by both spouses, but the woman retains responsibility for the household duties. In the *role-sharing* marriage, both spouses are employed, both are actively involved in parenting, and both share in the responsibilities and duties of the household.

Although neither Gilbert (1985) nor Peplau (1983) actually defines relationship equality, both seem to agree that there must be an equal sharing of power and equal investment in waged work in addition to the work of the home. Conversely, both also agree that partners who divide economic and domestic responsibilities on the basis of gender will be unable to achieve an equal relationship, even if this is their goal.

ꝫ Why Can't a Marriage Based on Separate Gender Roles Be Equal?

Separate gender roles undermine men's and women's ability to achieve an equal relationship in several mutually reinforcing ways. Separate gender roles limit wives' access to universally valued resources, give different meanings to the resources that husbands and wives contribute, and prescribe differences in men's and women's sense of entitlement.

Access to Resources

Power has been defined as the capacity to influence the behavior of others and to resist their influence on us (Bannester, 1969; Huston, 1983). Power is commonly viewed as emanating from a person's access to resources, but because a resource must be valued by the person whom one wishes to influence, the amount of power associated with any given resource is to some extent subjective. Certain resources, however, such as money, love, and prestige, are more universally valued than others (Foa & Foa, 1980).

Resources can be personal (e.g., love and affection) or concrete (e.g., money). Personal resources tend to be restricted in terms of the number of people to whom they apply, whereas concrete resources are likely to hold a broader sway. Six types of resources, or power bases, (reward, coercive, legitimate, expert, referent, and informational), have been the most frequently studied (French & Raven, 1959; Raven, 1974; Raven & Kruglanski, 1970).

Reward power is based on the capacity to provide either concrete or personal outcomes that are perceived to be desirable. Over time, reward power is believed to enhance the attractiveness of the influencer. Coercive power, in contrast, is based on the ability to administer outcomes that are perceived to be negative. To be effective, coercive power requires surveillance and, over time, results in diminished attraction and alienation. Indeed, among the married, coercive power is associated with the most negative outcomes of any power base (Gray-Little & Burks, 1983).

Legitimate power is based on a mutual recognition of one partner's "right" to exercise the authority associated with his or her position or social role. Among the married, as we shall see, distinctly different rights and responsibilities are associated with men's provider and women's nurturer roles. Yet whatever the specifics, legitimate power has a *should* or *ought* component evolving from internalized values prescribing that one is entitled to exercise authority, and the other has an obligation to accept that authority.

Expert power is based on a recognition of another's special knowledge or abilities and is limited in scope to the influencer's areas of expertise. Informational power is based on the content of the message and is the only power base perceived to be independent of the person by whom it is exercised. Finally, referent power is based on our desire to identify with, or want to be like, another. Of the six power bases, referent power is associated with the most positive outcomes among the married (Gray-Little & Burks, 1983).

Each of these bases of power has been viewed as gender linked. Primarily as a result of men's and women's separate gender roles, men often have access to more resources overall and are more likely to have access to concrete and universally valued resources. Men have been seen as higher on reward, coercive, legitimate, expert, and informational power and to have greater access to income and prestige. Of the six most-investigated bases of power, referent power is the only one to which men and women are perceived as having equal access (Johnson, 1978). Indeed, according to husbands, referent power is the primary source of marital power for wives (Raven, Centers, & Rodrigues, 1975). Why is this so?

In the ideology of separate gender roles, women are primarily responsible for the home, for child rearing, and for emotion work or relationship maintenance. As a result, women develop primarily personal, relationship-specific resources. Men, in contrast, are primarily responsible for the financial support of the family. As a result, they are more likely to develop concrete, universally valued resources (primarily earning power and prestige). Access to relationship-specific resources (i.e., those traditionally ascribed to women) is associated with limited alternatives and greater relationship dependency. Access to resources that are valued outside the relationship (i.e., those traditionally ascribed to men) expands one's alternatives and increases one's bargaining power within the relationship (England & Farkas, 1986).

But paid employment is more than access to earning power. As we saw in Chapter 2, paid employment is also a source of independent identity, increased self-esteem, and enhanced social contacts. In addition, and as we saw in Chapter 3, work outside the home is more positively valued than work inside the home. Even among couples with the best of intentions, it is exceedingly difficult to remain impervious to the values of the larger society. Indeed, in a recent study comparing women with jobs, women with careers, and career women who chose to step out of the labor force while their children were young, it was found that the professional women who had chosen to stay home to care for their children had the lowest self-esteem of any of the three groups (Sholomskas & Axelrod, 1987).

When a wife is unemployed, her loss of financial independence, her access to limited and primarily relationship-specific resources, her absence of alternative sources of achievement, self-esteem, and affirmation, and the inevitable reduction in her bargaining power converge in ways that make it exceedingly difficult for her to interact with her spouse as an equal partner. This is true even among couples striving to minimize materialistic concerns.

Employment per se, however, hardly ensures equality. Having a job is not the same as having an equally high-paying job of equally high status. Nor is it the same as having equal responsibility to provide financially for the family. Although 61% of married women are now employed, wives are still more likely to work part-time, to earn less, and to be in lower-status jobs than their husbands. Furthermore, and as a number of studies have shown, even among dual-career couples in which wives hold high-status positions, "his" career is still likely to be considered more important than "hers." Indeed, a recent study of dual-career couples showed that husbands who earned more than their wives said that their careers were more important than their spouses' careers—and their wives agreed. Yet for women who earned significantly more than their husbands, neither they nor their husbands thought that her career was more important than his (Steil & Weltman, 1991). Why the asymmetry?

Separate Gender Roles and the
Sense of Entitlement

The ideology of separate gender roles ascribes different meanings to the waged work of husbands and wives. Sixty-two percent of married women with children under the age of 6 are now employed. Twenty-six percent of employed wives earn more than their husbands (Krafft, 1994). Yet wives' earnings are still considered secondary because a majority of the men and women in our society continue to endorse the husband's role as primary provider (Blumstein & Schwartz, 1983; Haas, 1986; Potuchek, 1992).

In 1974, a national survey found that for almost 80% of the adult population, being a man meant being a good provider (Yankelovich, 1974). In 1980, the U.S. Census discontinued the practice of automatically designating the man as the head of the household. Yet a series of studies published in the 1980s and 1990s show that a majority of men and women, including employed wives and their spouses, continue to view the husband as primarily responsible for providing for the financial security of the family. In 1989, a study of high-achieving, dual-career couples found that 68% of husbands and 52% of wives believed that earning income was solely the husband's responsibility (Vannoy-Hiller & Philliber, 1989). Other studies support this finding. More than half of employed husbands and employed wives report that men's ultimate responsibility is providing for the family and that husbands bear the primary obligation to work to provide that support (Haas, 1986; Perry-Jenkins & Crouter, 1990; Perry-Jenkins, Seery, & Crouter, 1992; Potuchek, 1992). Yet in couples in which either spouse endorses the male provider role, the husband is more powerful regardless of his partner's income (Blumstein & Schwartz, 1983).

For a man, the provider role carries the obligation to earn and provide for the family. These responsibilities, however, entitle him to put his career above his wife's, free him from a number of responsibilities at home, entitle him to a position of greater influence, and allow him to perceive the time he devotes to his paid work as an expression of family caring. Traditionally, it has also allowed husbands to feel entitled to their wives' undivided support because their provider role was primary to the families' well-being.

For women, separate gender roles preclude the view of a wife as either primary provider or coprovider. Working-class wives in full-time, unionized jobs provide almost half (45%) of the family income. Yet these wives are likely to be seen as secondary wage earners rather than coproviders (Thompson & Walker, 1989). In white middle-class families, wives are often viewed as working out of choice rather than necessity. As a result, wives' employment is often considered not as an aspect of family provision but as an opportunity for self-development.

African American wives have a longer history of waged work than European American wives. Prior to the 1970s, black wives were more likely to be employed, more likely to be employed full-time, and more likely to be employed independent of their husbands' income level or their parental status than were white wives. As a result, a black wife's employment is more likely to be seen by herself and her husband as an integral and normative component of her roles of wife and mother (Malson, 1983). Rather than conflicting with her nurturing responsibilities, employment is seen as part of being a good mother.

Yet on other measures there is little difference in the family attitudes of black and white women (Heiss, 1988). Black women are at least as likely to accept views that emphasize self-sacrifice and motherhood as are white women (Dugger, 1988), and studies show no differences in the extent to which black and white women endorse the importance of the husband as provider and the wife as homemaker, nurturer, and relationship maintainer. Black women and men seem, then, to be more likely than their white counterparts to view paid employment as consistent with the mothering role, but black women are no less likely than white women to emphasize the importance of husbands as providers and to see themselves as holding primary responsibility for the home and the children.

Further Implications
of Gender-Based Roles

The vast majority of women and men continue to endorse the importance of husband as provider and wife as nurturer, but both may be unaware of the implications of their endorsement. When the husband is viewed as the primary provider, his wife, even when she earns as much or more than her spouse, is not entitled to view her career as primary, is not entitled to absent herself from household work, and, unlike her husband, would be criticized for saying that her waged work kept her from her children. As a result, the vast majority of wives, even when they are employed, continue to perform a disproportionate amount of domestic work. Over 70% of wives do all or almost all of the family laundry, meal preparation, shopping, child care, gift buying, outside errands, dishwashing, and bill paying (Berheide, 1984; DeStefano & Colasanto, 1990). Husbands, in contrast, reportedly do more than wives on three tasks: minor home repairs, yard work, and car maintenance. Because many women's tasks are likely to be done on a daily basis, whereas most men's tasks are likely to be inter-mittent and discretionary, there is a significant difference in the number of hours that wives spend in household tasks relative to their husbands.

Huber and Spitze (1983) found that full-time housewives spent about 52 hours per week on household labor, employed wives about 26, and husbands about 11. Other reviews of the literature conclude that husbands overall do about 33% of what wives do around the home. Husbands of employed wives do about 37% of the household labor that their spouses do, with coprovider husbands doing somewhat more. Because employed wives do significantly less household work than unemployed wives, the 4% relative increase for husbands actually represents less than 10 minutes more per day. Hochschild (1989) concluded that wives spend about 15 hours longer per week on household tasks than husbands do. She labeled this phenomenon women's "second shift" and calculated that, over a year, the second shift is equivalent to an extra month of 24-hour days.

Black marriages have often been reported to be more egalitarian than white marriages. However, the difference in black, compared with white, husbands' contributions to domestic labor is small. Employed black husbands spent less than 1.5 hours more per week on household work than employed white husbands (Beckett & Smith, 1981). Employed black, middle-class, professional couples divide domestic work along gender lines. Fathers spend more time in maintenance work. Mothers spend more time in cleaning, food work, and child care. Finally, and similar to their white counterparts, black wives perform approximately two thirds of all household chores (Hossain & Roopnarine, 1993).

In both black and white families, husbands' involvement in child care follows a similar pattern. Husbands of employed wives have increased their availability to children, especially when the children are of preschool age (Pleck, 1985; Thompson & Walker, 1989). Thus, husbands and wives report contributing almost equal amounts to their children's education and socialization, but fathers spend less than one third of the time in solo care that mothers do, and mothers perform much more of the day-to-day physical care (Hochschild, 1989; Pleck, 1985). Among blacks, the findings are similar: Fathers provide about one third of the primary care (Hossain & Roopnarine, 1993).

Just as wives' having a job is not the same as having the responsibility for providing for the family, husbands' "helping" is not the same as being primarily responsible for the children. Baruch and Barnett (1986) found that 70% of a random sample of fathers were not responsible for (defined as remembering, planning, and scheduling) any child-care tasks, and an additional 22% were responsible for only one such task.

Attitudes about the wife's role as provider have important implications for the division of labor at home and for wives' psychological well-being. Perry-Jenkins et al. (1992) divided employed women into three groups: *coproviders*, who saw their income as important to the family and saw the provider role as equally shared; *ambivalent coproviders*, who admitted that the family was dependent on their incomes but were uncomfortable with the reality of shared economic responsibility; and *main-secondary providers*, who viewed their incomes as helpful but not vital to the family's well-being. Although none of the husbands shared the work of the home equally, husbands of both coprovider and ambivalent coprovider wives spent double the time in household tasks as other husbands, and coprovider wives experienced less depression than any other group.

Time Availability

Some might ask whether wives' disproportionate assumption of the responsibilities of the home is not offset by husbands' disproportionate time spent in the paid labor force. Because husbands spend more time in outside employment, could it be that they simply do not have the same amount of time as their wives to spend on household labor? This argument is unsupported by the empirical literature. Although there is some evidence that husbands decrease their household labor when their work demands increase (Biernat & Wortman, 1991), there is little evidence of the reverse. Husbands do not increase their participation in household labor in any significant way when their work demands decrease.

The reverse is true for women. According to Pleck (1985), wives reduce their family time relatively little when employed, and wives who are employed the same number of hours as their husbands nonetheless perform much more family work. Even if a husband is unemployed, he does much less housework than a wife who puts in a 40-hour week. According to Blumstein and Schwartz (1983), this is the case even among couples who profess egalitarian ideals, including equal sharing of the work that has to be done in the house.

A Matter of Choice

Others may view the traditional division of labor as a matter of conscious choice made out of concern for what works best for the family. Yet there is growing evidence that the allocation of domestic responsibilities along gender lines and women's difficulty in having their careers valued equally is less a matter of conscious choice than a manifestation of internalized gender expectations.

Silberstein (1992), in an interview study of white professional dual-career couples, found that almost all men and women felt that it would be easier for the wives' careers to be less successful than the husbands' than for the reverse. Among the reasons the wives gave for this disparity were (a) his work was more important to his sense of self, (b) she needed her husband to be successful, and (c) she feared that people would say his lack of success was her fault for making him help at home.

Dual-career couples, it seems, "build life structures with one foot in the past, mimicking traditional marriages of their parents' generation, and one foot in the feminist influenced present . . . ." (Silberstein, 1992, p. 174). They hold not only "consciously altered expectations (about gender roles, work, family, and marriage) but also deeply socialized, internalized, and probably change resistant experiences, emotional needs and entrenched patterns of behavior" (p. 13). The result of that foot in the past is that work is considered more important to men than to women and that family is considered more important to women than to men.

The Sense of Entitlement and the Matter of Meaning

Studies have found that the higher a husband's earnings, the better he reports he is doing in both his parental and his spousal roles, but the greater a wife's earnings relative to her husband, the worse she says she feels about herself as a spouse (Biernat & Wortman, 1991). Other research has shown that couples will go to great lengths to conceal a high-earning wife's income to protect the husband's status as primary provider (Hochschild, 1989). Biernat and Wortman (1991) found that when academic women earned more than their partners, their husbands did *less* child care than did the husbands of wives who earned less than their partners. After eliminating a number of possible explanations, the authors concluded that the high-earning wives "absolved" their husbands from child-care responsibilities to compensate for the negative feelings evoked by their high salaries. This pattern is not restricted to whites. Aldous (1969) found that black working-class men whose wives worked performed fewer family tasks than those whose wives were home full-time.

Other studies show that women in nontraditional managerial and professional positions are more likely to become divorced, leave the labor force, or move to a lower-status position than women in traditional jobs; this pattern is more salient when the wife's position is similar in status to her husband's than when it is of lower status (Vannoy-Hiller & Philliber, 1989). Findings such as these make sense only in the context of a continued internalization of separate gender roles that ascribes different meanings to the waged and unwaged work of husbands and wives even among the most contemporary couples.

❧ Power Assessed by Performance of Domestic Work

Women's disproportionate investment in the work of the home is generally viewed as a major indicator of relationship inequality. This disproportionate investment increases wives' relationship-specific investments relative to their husbands', limits their access to more universally valued resources, restricts their alternatives, and reduces their bargaining power. The arrival of children, marking the apex of women's nurturing responsibilities, is strongly associated with the reactivation of traditional roles even among previously egalitarian couples. The concomitant loss of wives' sense of entitlement brings secondary costs in terms of fatigue, loss of self-esteem, further reductions in relationship equality, and increased marital dissatisfaction.

The allocation of domestic work is most frequently assessed by self-report measures. One or both spouses are asked to indicate the extent to which specific household or child-care tasks are performed "entirely" or "primarily" by the husband, by the wife, or by "husband and wife equally." In the late 1960s, family sociologists also began to employ time-use methods (Pleck, 1985) in which respondents were asked to keep detailed diaries of time spent on a variety of activities over specified weekday and weekend periods.

Across both time and task measurement strategies, the findings are the same. In the vast majority of homes, allocation of domestic work continues to be divided along gender lines, such that wives, even when they are employed and even when they earn more than husbands, continue to perform a disproportionate amount of the work of the home. Most studies conclude that employed wives continue to do approximately 64% of the total housework, and although there is considerable variability in the asymmetries, estimates of the percent of husbands in dual-earner families who share the work of the home equally range from a low of less than 2% to a high of 12% (Ferree, 1991; Nyquist, Slivken, Spence, & Helmreich, 1985).

⤖ Power Assessed as Say in Decision Making

In addition to studying the allocation of domestic work, power has also been measured as say in decision making. Measures of decision-making say achieved particular prominence in the 1960s, when Blood and Wolfe (1960), in a singularly influential study, undertook to assess the social structure of families on the basis of the power positions of husbands and wives. A sample of 731 urban and suburban wives and 178 farm wives were asked "who usually makes the final decision about" eight areas of family life. The eight decision areas were purportedly selected to meet the criteria of importance, universality, and, reflecting an endorsement of separate gender roles, representativeness of masculine versus feminine spheres. The eight areas included who makes the final decision regarding what job the husband should take, who makes the final decision regarding whether or not the wife should go to work or quit work, and who decides how much money the family can afford to spend per week on food.

Husbands were nine times as likely to have the final say over their own job and twice as likely to have the final say regarding their wife's work as they were to have the final say on the food budget. This shows that although some studies of decision making assess relative power, others assess only the more powerful partner's willingness to relinquish or delegate say in areas that are time consuming and considered less critical (Safilios-Rothschild, 1969). These are clearly two different concepts. Some investigators have addressed this discrepancy by using a number of decision-making areas and asking respondents to indicate not only who has the major say in each area but also the relative importance of each area (Blumstein & Schwartz, 1983). Still others have used more global assessments, asking, "When there's a really important decision on which you two are likely to disagree, who usually wins out?" (Heer, 1962), or simply, "Who has the final say in major decisions?"

All of these measures are based on self-report. In addition, all focus on the outcome of decision making while neglecting the process (Lips, 1981). Yet as we saw in Chapter 2, although equal decision making was associated with relationship satisfaction, within that context, decisions made jointly by both partners were associated with greater satisfaction than those made separately (Gray-Little & Burks, 1983).

Who Has the Power?

With these caveats, what do the studies show? In 1960, 90% of the husbands in Blood and Wolfe's study reportedly had the final say regarding their own job, whereas only 39% of the wives had the final say regarding whether they should or should not work. Conversely, 1% of wives had the final say regarding their husband's job, but 26% of husbands had the final say regarding their wife's employment. In 1972, Turk and Bell asked a sample of 336 Canadian households, "Who is the real boss in your family?" Seventy-six percent of wives responded that the husband was the boss, compared to only 13% who responded that power was equally shared.

In the early '80s a national survey of cohabitating or married heterosexual and homosexual couples found that lesbian couples were the only ones in which partners' relative earnings were not an important determinant of decision-making say (Blumstein & Schwartz, 1983). Employed wives were less likely to report husband dominance in decision making than were unemployed wives. Approximately 60% of the respondents overall reported having relatively equal say in decision making. For dual-career couples, the percent of those reporting relatively equal say was even higher. Yet even in dual-career couples in which wives earned significantly more than their husbands, husbands were likely to maintain greater say in financial matters (Steil & Weltman, 1991).

ᔌ Power Assessed as Influence Strategy Use

Earlier in this chapter, we noted that power is defined as the ability to influence others while resisting their influence on ourselves. We also noted that power is based on one's access to resources. The number and kinds of valued resources to which one has access is believed to be associated with the way influence is exercised. People who are self-confident and who have access to concrete and more universally valued resources (e.g., status, money, and knowledge) use direct and interactive (or bilateral) modes of influence. They are more likely to openly state their desires and to use reason, logic, and mutual talk to influence others. Those who are less self-confident and who do not have access to concrete and highly valued resources are more likely to rely on personal (e.g., attractiveness, liking) and helpless bases of power and to use indirect and noninteractive (or unilateral) modes of influence (Instone, Major, & Bunker, 1983; Johnson, 1978). Those with little access to resources are more likely to use strategies such as hinting, crying, clamming up, withdrawing, or bullying to influence others.

Although any mode of influence can be effective in the short run, in the long run there are significant differences in the outcomes associated with different kinds of strategy use. People using direct and rational strategies are perceived by others to be more socially skilled (Falbo, 1977), more self-confident and influential, and more effective as leaders (Izraeli, 1987) than people using strategies labeled as indirect or manipulative. In comparison, people using indirect, helpless, and personal modes of influence are believed to suffer negative consequences in terms of dependence, lowered self-esteem, and subordinated positions (Johnson, 1978). Consistent with this view, direct strategies have been shown to be the strategies of choice for women and men alike, whereas indirect or manipulative strategies are consistently ranked as the strategies of last resort (Steil & Hillman, 1993; White & Roufail, 1989).

During the last decade, a number of investigators examined the strategies that men and women use in their close relationships. In one of the earliest and most influential studies, 200 unmarried homosexual and heterosexual university students were asked to think about their intimate partner and write an open-ended essay describing "how I get _____ (my partner) to do what I want" (Falbo & Peplau, 1980). Findings showed that, among heterosexuals, men reported using direct and bilateral strategies more often than did women, whereas women reported using indirect and unilateral strategies more often than did men. There were no differences in the self-reported use of influence strategies among those in homosexual relationships, but overall and regardless of relationship type, people who perceived themselves as having more power than their partners were also more likely to use bilateral and direct strategies. Studies of cohabiting or married gay but not lesbian partners have shown similar findings. Those who have fewer resources than their partners and who are in relationships with men are more likely to use indirect strategies such as manipulation and supplication as means of influence (Howard, Blumstein, & Schwartz, 1986).

Other studies have found no differences by sex in the self-reported use of direct strategies (Howard, Blumstein, & Schwartz,

1986). Aida and Falbo (1991) looked at influence strategy use in a sample of 42 married couples divided into two groups: *egalitarians*, defined as those couples in which the spouses regarded themselves as equally responsible for providing financially for the family, and *traditionals*, defined as those couples who saw the husband as responsible for providing financially. Egalitarians were more satisfied with their relationships and reported a greater likelihood of confiding and showing affection than traditionals. There were no differences by couple type in terms of the kinds of strategies (direct, indirect, unilateral, and bilateral) used. Traditionals, particularly wives in traditional relationships, used more strategies overall than did egalitarians.

Steil and Weltman (1992) examined the extent to which sex, resources, social roles, and individual differences in self-confidence, nurturance, and achievement striving were associated with influence strategy use among a sample of 60 professional dual-career couples. To control for sex-linked differences in access to resources, respondents were recruited so that in half the couples the women earned at least one third more than their husbands. For the other half of the sample the income discrepancy was reversed, so that the husbands earned at least one third more than their wives. Primarily as a result of these selection criteria, there were no differences between men and women in terms of job prestige, income, and self-confidence. Nor were there any differences in the extent to which they described themselves as nurturant and affiliative, or oriented toward autonomy, dominance, and achievement.

Consistent with the literature's predictions for such a highly achieving sample, the strategy most frequently used by both men and women was the direct request. For both husbands and wives, more frequent use of indirect strategies was associated with lower self-confidence and with less power at home, as measured by say in financial matters.

Finally, the findings of all studies show that, regardless of sexual orientation or relationship type, use of direct-bilateral strategies is associated with higher levels of relationship intimacy and satisfaction, and use of indirect and unilateral strategies is associated with lower levels of relationship intimacy and greater dissatisfaction

(Aida & Falbo, 1991; Falbo & Peplau, 1980; Rosenbluth & Steil, 1995).

❧ Summary of the Decision-Making, Task-Sharing, and Influence Strategy Literature

What do these findings tell us? First, it is clear that the predominant theory underlying all the studies is that power is based on access to resources. For men, the findings consistently support resource predictions. For men in both homosexual and heterosexual relationships, the more they earned relative to their partners, the greater their say in decision making, the lower their involvement in domestic work, and, for heterosexual men, the better they felt about themselves as spouses. Also consistent with resource predictions, heterosexual women and gay men who had fewer resources than their male partners were more likely to use weaker modes of influence, such as supplication and manipulation.

For women, support for the resource position is less consistent. Employed wives did have greater say in marital decision making than unemployed wives, but husbands of employed women did not significantly increase their participation in domestic tasks, and women who earned significantly more than their husbands did not have equal say in financial matters. Moreover, women who earned more than their husbands did not feel better about themselves as spouses, and for some, their husbands actually did less at home. Thus, access to broadly valued resources, such as income and job prestige, did not result in the same outcomes for wives as for husbands.

In addition, earnings relative to one's spouse were not predictive of decision making say for women in lesbian relationships, and, unlike those in heterosexual and gay male relationships, access to fewer resources was not associated with increased use of low-power strategies, such as manipulation and supplication. The differences in the findings for women in relationships with women, compared to women and men in relationships with men, are consistent with the notion that power has gendered meanings.

Women, it is said, regard power in terms of responsibility and care for others. Thus, they use power to foster growth and enhance the power of others (Miller, 1986). Men, on the other hand, are more likely to perceive power in terms of assertion, aggression, and achievement (McClelland, 1975) and are more likely to use power to advance themselves by controlling, limiting, or destroying the power of others (Miller, 1986). This view of power, it is said, leads men, who have learned in the workplace that money equals power, to impose this same equation at home (Blumstein & Schwartz, 1983).

And what of influence strategy use? Studies consistently showed that direct and, particularly, direct-bilateral strategies are preferred by both women and men. Furthermore, direct-bilateral strategies are the strategies of choice for those who see themselves as powerful and confident. Indirect strategies are less preferred and are used more frequently by those who have fewer resources, less self-confidence, and less say than their partners. For men and women, lack of power was associated with indirect strategy use. Men, however, more frequently used noninteractive strategies, such as withdrawing. Women, consistent with the nurturing and relationship maintenance aspects of their gender role, seemed to use more interactive strategies, such as smiling and suggesting.

Despite these differences, the association between influence strategy use and relationship outcomes was clear and consistent. Across all studies, strategies reflecting an imbalance of power between the partners were associated with negative outcomes, whereas those associated with a more equal balance of power were associated with positive outcomes. Indirect strategy use was associated with more dissatisfaction and less intimacy. Direct-bilateral strategy use and perceptions of equality were associated with the highest levels of relationship satisfaction and the highest levels of relationship intimacy.

⭐ Other Social Science Perspectives

Two other groups of scholars, who hold opposing viewpoints, have written extensively on equality in close relationships. Drawing their hypotheses from the resource position, exchange theorists define equality in terms of equal outcomes. Coming from a more psychodynamic and clinical perspective, mutuality theorists reject the exchange position and emphasize the importance of process.

Equality as Equal Outcomes: The Exchange Perspective

Exchange theorists assess the relative equality of a relationship by asking respondents to rate their own and their partners' relationship contributions and outcomes across a variety of areas that typically include (a) personal characteristics (e.g., attractiveness, sociability, intelligence); (b) emotional concerns (e.g., love, understanding, commitment); (c) day-to-day exchanges (e.g., earning money, maintaining the house, fitting in with friends and relatives); and (d) opportunities gained and lost (e.g., having children, the opportunity to marry others). Relationships are defined as *equal* when the outcomes that both partners receive are the same regardless of their contributions (Cate, Lloyd, & Henton, 1985; Cate, Lloyd, Henton, & Larson, 1982; Martin, 1985; Micheals, Edwards, & Acock, 1984). Relationships are defined as *equitable* when each receives outcomes proportionate to his or her partner's, relative to what each has contributed. Thus, partners are entitled to receive desired outcomes and to avoid undesired outcomes in proportion to what each has contributed to the relationship relative to the other. Finally, *need-based* relationships are defined as those in which people are entitled to what they need regardless of what they've contributed. Unlike the other positions presented in this chapter, exchange theorists endorse equity, rather than equality, as the appropriate basis for an intimate relationship (Walster, Walster, & Berscheid, 1978).

According to the exchange perspective, equity and equality can sometimes overlap. If both partners contribute equal amounts of valued resources and have equal costs, then both are entitled to the same outcomes, and equity and equality are synonymous. If the contributions of the two partners differ but their outcomes are the same, the relationship is equal but not equitable. If contributions differ but outcomes are proportionate, the relationship is equitable but not equal.

Consistent with the predictions of exchange theorists, studies based on the assessment of inputs and outcomes have found that equity and equality are highly correlated. In one study, equitable outcomes overlapped with equal outcomes in as many as 70% of the cases (Cate et al., 1982). In another, equity and equality correlated more strongly with each other than did global and summed measures of equity alone, thereby raising serious methodological concerns (Micheals et al., 1984). How can measures of two different constructs (equity and equality) be more highly correlated with each other than global, compared to summed measures of the same construct (i.e., equity). What is really being measured? Equity? Equality? Or simply an artifact of the measurement strategies?

Other scholars have criticized the exchange approach for its short-term perspective and its failure to consider process. Equality, they argue, involves the perception of a mutual give-and-take over the long term rather than an immediate comparison of specific outcomes (Deutsch, 1985). From this perspective, equality should be unrelated to equity but closely related to need. Need, particularly reciprocal need, is perceived to be closely linked to equality because both share an orientation toward reciprocity over the long term and both are governed by the norms of communal (i.e., family) rather than exchange (i.e., business) relationships (Williamson & Clark, 1989).

When equity and equality are assessed using methodologies other than those used by exchange theorists, the findings are quite different. Consistent with those who emphasize the importance of process, studies show that those in equality, compared to equity, conditions are more likely to say that *both* parties, rather than only one or the other, initiate decision-making issues, and *both* are more likely to benefit. In addition, empirical findings show that men and women prefer equality to equity as the basis for decision making in intimate relationships, and that they report more positive feelings about the decision, themselves, and their partners when equality rather than equity is used (Steil & Makowski, 1989).

Equality as Mutuality

Mutuality theorists also reject the exchange orientation for its failure to consider process. Representing a more clinical and psychodynamic orientation, Benjamin (1988) describes equal relationships as those in which two individuals participate in mutual exchange and mutual recognition. One is both affecting the other and being affected by the other. There is an openness to influence and emotional availability (Jordan, 1986). Each responds to the other in a way that makes the feelings, intentions, and actions of the other meaningful. Both parties have and express desires, both parties are active and empowered, and the relationship is characterized by mutual respect (Benjamin, 1988). Both partners put attention and energy into caring not only for the well-being of the other but also for the relationship itself (Jordan, 1986; McAdams, 1988; McClelland, 1975). Mutuality, from this perspective and in opposition to the exchange theorists, involves a shared sense of relationship that transcends the immediate and reciprocal exchange of benefits (Genero, Miller, Surrey, & Baldwin, 1992).

Those who emphasize mutuality assert that equal, compared to unequal, relationships are more likely to lead to the psychological development of both partners (Miller, 1986). Equal relationships are experienced as energizing and empowering and foster a sense of self-worth and connectedness. Indeed, according to many, ideal intimacy can be achieved only in relationships that are equal (McAdams, 1988; Rubin, 1983).

Unequal relationships are those in which one partner is likely to dominate another. Unequal relationships are believed to undermine the basis of mutual and self-respect by signifying that the participants do not have the same value. Rather than increasing openness and understanding, unequal relationships are characterized by deception and manipulation. Subordinates resort to disguised and indirect ways of acting and reacting, and there is reciprocal condescension (Miller, 1986).

Mutuality theory is recent and only beginning to be studied empirically. Findings from studies by investigators of other theoretical orientations, however, are consistent with the mutuality position. Earlier in this chapter we saw that those in relationships where there was an imbalance of power were more likely to use indirect and manipulative modes of influence. In Chapter 3, we saw that dominant partners in unequal relationships, that is, those who perceive themselves as controlling decision making, rated themselves more favorably than they did their partners and were less attracted to, less satisfied, and less happy with their relationships than were those in relationships where decision making was equally shared. Finally, in one of the few studies directly testing these ideas, mutuality was associated with greater relationship satisfaction and cohesion and less depression for men and women alike (Genero et al., 1992).

❧ Relationship Equality: What Does It Mean to Couples Themselves?

The variety of perspectives on relationship equality, demonstrated by the literature reviewed in this chapter, is testimony to the difficulty social scientists have in defining and operationalizing the term. How, we wonder, do laymen and laywomen conceptualize equality? To what extent are their conceptualizations consistent with those of scholars who study relationships? To what extent do the measures that social scientists use reflect respondents' experience of equality in their own marriages?

In a study specifically designed to address these questions (Rosenbluth et al., in press), husbands and wives in dual-career couples were asked to think of couples they knew whose marriages they considered to be either equal or unequal and to describe why they characterized the relationships in those terms. They were also asked, through both open- and closed-ended questions, what they believed to be the most important or central aspects of marital equality. Thus, some questions explicitly asked the respondents to consider equality and inequality in others' relationships, whereas other questions required respondents to think about equality in a more self-referential way.

Respondents in this study were white, urban, upper middle-class professionals who had been married about 5 years and were, on average, 32 years old. They were highly educated. Over 80% of the respondents and their spouses held advanced degrees, and all worked in relatively prestigious careers, primarily in business, medicine, and law.

Contrary to investigator expectations, the men and women expressed many similar views about marital equality. Overall, they endorsed marital equality as "very important" in their own marriages and described themselves as relating to their spouses as equals relatively frequently. Yet even for this sample, considerable asymmetries prevailed. Although 17% of the wives earned more than their husbands, none of the wives' careers was considered primary. Indeed, despite the fact that the male and female respondents had comparable careers, half (51%) considered the wives' careers less important than the husbands', and over half (54%) reported that wives retained primary responsibility for homemaking tasks.[1]

Task Division

Domestic task division was the most frequently cited criterion for why respondents considered relationships other than their own to be equal or unequal. When asked to think about a married couple whose relationship was equal, a male respondent said, "They both have important, demanding jobs and they share pretty much equally in the home and child-care duties."

Similarly, when asked what made them think of a relationship as unequal, respondents most frequently described an asymmetrical division of responsibilities. A female respondent described a couple whose "marriage is unequal because the wife has much more responsibility for the marriage and the home and doesn't think it's appropriate to challenge it. She's a career woman and just assumes those responsibilities. She's content with what I think of as real inequality."

Relationship Characteristics

When respondents were asked one of the more self-referential questions, "How would you define equality in a marital relationship," the equitable division of tasks was superseded by relationship characteristics. Mutual respect, commitment, supportiveness, and reciprocity over time were the relationship characteristics most frequently associated with a perception of equality. In the words of one respondent, "There's a sense of shared responsibility. That doesn't mean that every responsibility is equally shared but that there's a splitting up of what's necessary to maintain the relationship and an overall state of well-being." Another respondent described an equal relationship as one with

> a constant give and take. There's a tremendous mutual respect. Sometimes one is the leader, sometimes the other is the leader. They have a good sense of space for each other and they also have excellent communication in terms of their ability to work out issues over time in a way that is satisfactory to them both.

Capturing the essential attitude underlying many of these responses, one respondent said, "It's a frame of mind, looking at each other as equals and considering each other's opinions equally."

Decision Making

Decision making was mentioned or endorsed with moderate frequency across all measures. Interestingly, however, it was twice as likely to be mentioned when absent, as a feature of unequal relationships, than when present, as a feature of equal relationships.

Economic Resources

The reverse was true of economic resources. Contrary to the resource theory perspective, economic resources were raised infrequently or not at all. Economic resources were rarely mentioned as an indicator of inequality, but similarity of spouses' economic resources and contributions was noted by a third of the respondents in their descriptions of equality.

Advantages and Disadvantages of Equal Marriages

Both men and women generated a greater number of advantages than disadvantages of equal marriages. The most frequently mentioned advantage was enhancement of the marital relationship (25% of responses), which had greater stability and less conflict, less dependency, and less resentment.

As one female respondent noted,

> there's less stress, because one doesn't feel, "Hey, I'm doing all this and you're not doing anything." And when you have to do things at home, it doesn't really bother you because you know that your spouse is doing something that's equal in terms of time commitment.

According to a male respondent, equal marriages are "healthier because equality makes people feel better about each other and themselves."

Decreased stress due to shared labor, increased opportunities for personal development, equal value given to goals and contributions, shared decision making, shared experiences, and benefit to children were also seen as advantages of marital equality. As one man explained, "I think it's better for children to see that their father helps out around the house and that their mother has a respectable job . . . has another life outside the home."

The most frequently raised disadvantage, cited by almost half of the respondents (45%), was the negative effect that equality can have on marital relationships by requiring daily negotiations and compromise: "All the decisions are harder because everything has to be decided by both people." Several respondents mentioned that maintaining complete equality, if indeed possible, would require constant "bookkeeping," forcing family life to become too "businesslike." The idea of "keeping score" seemed to clash with respondents' sense of what marriage should be like. As one woman put it, "I think you can get very picky, like it's my day to do this and it's your day to do that."

Almost a quarter of the sample cited the burdens that equality imposes on husbands, including a loss of power, participation in the family in unfamiliar ways that might conflict with masculine identity, and interference with career demands. As one man said, "It would be a lot easier to be the dominant partner and have your spouse make all the compromises and sacrifices." Another noted that "The cost of being equal is the sacrifice that you need to make at work, either in promotional opportunity, salary increases, or whatever."

Summary of the Findings

This study was based on a convenience sample of highly educated, professional, dual-career respondents. Thus it cannot be said that they are representative of dual-career couples in general, nor are they representative of the spectrum of partners in dual-earner, compared with dual-career, families.[2] Yet with these caveats, what do the findings suggest?

First, it seems that when asked to consider the relationships of others, these dual-career respondents relied on behavioral criteria as do professional researchers. They most frequently described marriages as equal when they observed that domestic tasks and responsibilities were shared. Shared decision making, the area in which the most significant gains have been achieved, was noted primarily when absent. In contrast, equality of earning power, which is less common, was only notable when present. Equal participation in task sharing, an issue with which all couples struggle on a daily basis, was noted in both its presence and its absence.

Second, and consistent with mutuality theory, when responding to questions that reflected on their own relationships, respondents were more likely to cite the importance of feelings of mutual respect, supportiveness, commitment, and reciprocity over time, rather than concrete behaviors such as task division. In fact, when asked whether a marriage in which both spouses work full-time but one does most of the household and child care tasks is necessarily unequal, almost two thirds said no, such a marriage is not necessarily unequal. Different criteria seemed to be salient when respondents were evaluating the relationships of others compared to their own. How can we explain this?

Several non–mutually exclusive explanations are possible. First, one has more information about one's own relationship than the relationships of others. Thus, attitudes of mutual respect and reciprocity over time may be easier to assess in one's own marriage than in the marriages of others. Second, as previous chapters have suggested, household tasks performed in a context of reciprocal support and appreciation may feel less like tasks that a person of lower status is performing for a person of higher status, and an organically shared sense of family commitment may be more emotionally satisfying than evenly split domestic responsibilities. Third, the discrepancy in criteria may reflect the conflicts that partners in dual-career relationships experience in a time of transition and change and the particular difficulties they encounter in their attempts to achieve equal sharing in a societal context that continues to operate under the ideology of separate gender roles. Despite a general tendency to endorse equality, only a minority of these respondents were actually in relationships in which tasks were equally shared and careers were equally valued. Assessing their own relationships in terms of behavioral criteria would inevitably make salient the gap between their egalitarian ideals and the reality of their relationships. To what extent, then, does diverting the focus from objective, behavioral criteria to subjective relationship characteristics facilitate coping with inequality when equality is the stated ideal?

Finally, participants' responses to our open-ended queries about the disadvantages of equality included specific rejections of an exchange orientation. Several objected to a bookkeeping mentality that makes a communal relationship too businesslike. Indeed, research findings support the respondents' concerns. Murstein, Cerreto, and MacDonald (1977) found that an exchange orientation was associated with poor marital adjustment, and Fromm (1956) suggested that love relations in which market concerns prevail are often flawed.

⁊ Conclusions

So how should equality be defined? Should it be defined in terms of behavioral criteria, such as equal involvement in household tasks, child care, paid employment and decision making? Should it be defined in terms of equal outcomes? As equal opportunity for equal outcomes? As reciprocity over time? Should it be defined in terms of process, such as having an equal voice in decision making? Should it be defined in terms of attitudes, such as mutual respect and mutual commitment to the relationship? Or, in the final analysis, is equality a multi- rather than unidimensional construct involving not one, but all, of these components?

Merriam-Webster's *Collegiate Dictionary* defines equal as being of "identical value." Equal relationships require equal valuing: equal value given to each partner's aspirations and abilities, each partner's desires, concerns, and needs; equal valuing of each partner's work; and equal valuing of the relationship itself. Equal valuing is an attitude, and like all attitudes it must have not only cognitive but also affective and behavioral components. Equal valuing requires a context of equal power. As the research reviewed here shows, equal power between men and women cannot be achieved in the context of separate gender roles.

We began this chapter with a series of questions about relationship equality. What is it? How should it be defined? Why does it matter? This volume proposes that relationship equality is a matter of attitudes and behaviors and process. Relationship equality involves equal participation in the responsibilities of the home, equal commitment to the responsibility to provide, equal voice in establishing priorities, and equal commitment to and investment in the work of relationships. And, yes, equality matters. Inequality is costly to the less powerful partner in terms of increased dependency, lowered self-esteem, and more frequent feelings of hostility and depression. Inequality is costly to the more powerful partner in terms of decreased openness, loss of intimacy, and decreased relationship satisfaction. Equality, as we have seen, is associated with greater relationship satisfaction, more direct and mutual modes of influence, and increased intimacy for both partners. As we will see in the next chapter, intimacy is strongly related to both husbands' and wives' well-being.

ᐓ Notes

1. Using criteria similar to those of Peplau (1983) and Gilbert (1985), respondents' relationships were categorized into one of three family types: (a) *egalitarian,* couples who stated that their careers were equally valued and

homemaking tasks were equally shared, (b) *traditional,* couples who stated that the husband's career was primary and the wife was primarily responsible for homemaking, and (c) *transitional,* couples who stated that either the husband's career was primary and the couple shared homemaking tasks equally, or the wife was primarily responsible for homemaking and their careers were equally valued. Of the respondents, 32.5% were categorized as traditional, 40% as transitional, and 27.5% as egalitarian.

Five years later we did a follow-up study (Steil, Leonardo, & Whitcomb, in preparation). Thirty-six of the original 41 respondents were contacted. Twenty-nine (69%) responded. Those who responded included 12 men and 13 women, and there were no differences in the response rates of those who had originally been categorized as traditionals, transitionals, or egalitarians. At time two, all but one of the respondents had children. Only 8% of respondents at time two were in egalitarian relationships, 46% were in transitional relationships, and 46% were in traditional relationships. Thirteen respondents were in the same relationship type at time one and time two, whereas two reported being in a more egalitarian relationship and eight reported being in a more traditional relationship.

2. Most investigators differentiate between dual-career and dual-earner families. The differentiating criterion is the extent to which partners view their paid work as a job or a career. Paid work is defined as a career rather than a job to the extent that it requires special education and training, is cast in terms of achievement and continued advancement, and is viewed as a life's work.

5

Intimacy, Emotion Work, and Husbands' and Wives' Well-Being

Socio-emotional support from significant others . . . appears to be the most powerful predictor of reduced psychological distress [and] disorder . . . .

Thoits, 1985, p. 54

[Conceptualizing] "emotional support" as intimacy overlooks the fact that marriage and family as institutions do not just spontaneously occur . . . but require work, including emotion work.

Erickson, 1993, p. 890

Self-disclosure, emotional expressiveness, affirmation, acceptance, and affection are all important aspects of relationships that contribute to the well-being of the partners. Traditionally, these relationship qualities have been viewed as natural outcomes of intimacy benefiting both partners equally. More recent constructions emphasize that these qualities are the result of *emotion work,* defined as the *efforts* partners make to understand each other and to empathize with the other's situation and feelings (England & Farkas, 1986). From this latter perspective, qualities such as emotional expressiveness, affirmation, and acceptance are achieved rather than natural, and, as shown in this chapter, are often a source of relationship inequality associated with gender differences in well-being.

✷ Characteristics of Intimacy

Despite many attempts to define intimacy, there is no single definition on which all agree. There are, however, a number of defining characteristics on which there is some consensus. First, intimacy is interpersonal, taking place between two or more people. Individuals, however, differ in their capacity and motivation for intimacy, and this may influence the level of relational intimacy that is desired or achieved. Second, intimacy is reciprocal; it is "generated not by unilateral desire . . . but . . . by mutual consent" (Sexton & Sexton, 1982). Intimacy involves "reciprocal expression of feeling[s] and thought[s], . . out of a wish to know another's inner life and to be able to share one's own" (Rubin, 1983, p. 90). Third, relationship intimacy has cognitive, affective, and behavioral components. Intimates are willing to reveal themselves to one another, care deeply about one another, and are comfortable in close proximity (Hatfield & Rapson, 1987).

Self-disclosure, the sharing of private thoughts, dreams, beliefs, and emotionally meaningful experiences (Waring, Tillman, Frelick, Russell, & Weisz, 1980; Wynne & Wynne, 1986), is often viewed as synonymous with intimacy. For a relationship to be intimate, however, self-disclosure must occur in a context of appreciation, affection, understanding, and acceptance (Helgeson, Shaver, & Dyer, 1987; Reis & Shaver, 1988; Wynne & Wynne, 1986). According to some, an intimate experience has not taken place until there is empathic feedback—until acceptance and acknowledgment are communicated, verbally or nonverbally, as an indication that trust is justified. Fourth, then, intimacy is validating.

Intimate Relationships Versus Intimate Experiences

Intimate relationships build on but are more than a collection of intimate experiences. Intimate *experiences* are characterized by feelings of closeness and perceived understanding that partners experience along with, or as a result of, sharing that which is personal or private with each other (Prager, 1995). Intimate experiences are often unpredictable and spontaneous (Schaeffer & Olson, 1981). They may be a one-time occurrence involving no future commitments (for example, the stranger on the plane who tells you his or her life story). Intimate *relationships* involve the sharing of close experiences across a range of areas that may include the intellectual, emotional, social, and recreational (Schaeffer & Olson, 1981). In contrast to the unpredictable and spontaneous nature of intimate experiences, intimate relationships are those in which intimate interactions occur on a regular or predictable basis (Prager, 1995). Intimate relationships require mutual commitment to the other and to the relationship. They take time to develop and effort to maintain (Schaeffer & Olson, 1981).

Intimacy as Process

Intimacy is sometimes viewed as a process in itself, but it is really a corollary of other basic relationship processes, including a mutual willingness to express and attend and to understand and affirm. Expression and attention need not always be verbal, and understanding and affirmation need not imply agreement. But for intimacy to develop, all must take place in a context of empathic understanding. In the absence of empathy, attempts at intimate support often miss the mark. Partners may address one concern while ignoring, denying, or failing to perceive others (Thoits, 1985). When people disclose they seek a comparable response (Brehm, 1992). Those making emotional disclosures usually want an emotional response. Those making pragmatic or factual disclosures often want a factual response. In the absence of empathy, emotional concerns may be met with pragmatic or problem-solving responses, or, conversely, pragmatism may be met with emotion. Mismatched responses leave the discloser feeling misunderstood and devalued rather than affirmed, and under these conditions intimacy will suffer.

Relationship intimacy is never completed or fully accomplished but develops, fluctuates, and changes over time (Acitelli & Duck, 1987; Schaeffer and Olson, 1981). Relationship intimacy must be continually affirmed through shared experiences in which partners feel understood and valued. Under these conditions, intimacy benefits both partners, enriching their relationship and promoting psychological and emotional growth. In the absence of understanding and validation, or through mere neglect, there can be stagnation and gradual deterioration, a diminution of shared experiences and a decline in appreciation and affection. Under such conditions, individuals can become "trapped in a totally impoverished relationship without even being able to recognize what happened or why" (Lynch, 1977, p. 224).

Intimate relationships involve vulnerability. They are based on trust, a belief that confidences will not be manipulated or betrayed. But confidences are sometimes betrayed, and trust is sometimes violated. As a result, although "intimacy empowers people to benefit one another, . . . it also provides a setting for duplicity, manipulation, and cruelty" (Reis, 1990, p. 26).[1]

ൖ Intimacy and Well-Being

Evidence of a relationship between the availability and quality of intimacy in a person's life and the level of psychological well-being that person experiences comes from at least four kinds of studies. The first are studies conducted primarily with college undergraduates. In one of the best-known examples, healthy undergraduate students wrote over four consecutive days about either trivial events or personally upsetting experiences (Pennebaker & Beale, 1986). Of those writing about upsetting experiences some were asked to concentrate their writing on the event itself without referring to their feelings, some were asked to describe their feelings, and some were instructed to both describe an upsetting event and report any feelings they had about it. Immediately after writing the essays, students reported having more negative moods and had somewhat higher blood pressure readings than before writing the essays. Yet a follow-up study 6 months later showed that those who described both a personally upsetting event *and* their feelings about it made fewer visits to the university health center during the 6 months following the essay writing than students who wrote about trivial events or students who described only the facts. Although the long-term decreases in health problems were most pronounced among students who wrote about both traumas and their resulting emotions, writing only about emotions also proved beneficial. Subsequent studies by Pennebaker and others have replicated and extended these findings (Pennebaker, Colder, & Sharp, 1990; Pennebaker, Kiecolt-Glaser, & Glaser, 1988). Talking, operationalized as speaking into a tape recorder, and writing about stressful events was associated with lower skin conductance levels (Pennebaker, Hughes, & O'Heeron, 1987) and positive immunological changes (Esterling, Antoni, Fletcher, Margulies, & Schneiderman, 1994). Indeed, those who verbally disclosed emotions associated with stressful or traumatic events showed more benefits than those who only wrote about them. Although studies of this type are not studies of intimacy per se, they do point to the benefits of emotional expression in a nonjudgmental context.

A second group of studies looked at the relationship between well-being and *intimacy motivation*, defined as "a recurrent preference or readiness for experiences of warm, close, and communicative interaction with others" (McAdams & Bryant, 1987, p. 395). People high in intimacy motivation value warm and reciprocal human interaction, share more personal information, and elicit more self-disclosure from their friends than individuals low in intimacy motivation. In a nationwide sample of over 1,200 adults, high intimacy motivation among women was associated with higher levels of reported happiness and satisfaction in work, marriage, and parenting roles. Among men, higher intimacy motivation was associated with lower levels of reported strain (defined as anxiety, ill health, or drug and alcohol abuse) and lower levels of uncertainty (defined as worry, doubt, and economic anxiety; McAdams & Bryant, 1987). In a longitudinal study, high intimacy motivation measured at age 30 among a sample of Harvard graduates was strongly associated with higher levels of psychosocial adjustment, including marital happiness, 17 years later (McAdams & Vaillant, 1982).

A third group of studies equates intimacy with marital status. As reported in Chapter 1, these studies generally show a positive relationship between marriage and psychological well-being for both women and men but particularly for men.

The fourth and final group of intimacy and well-being studies look beyond marital status per se to the quality of couple interactions. Men who reported that they felt a lack of emotional support from their wives were far more likely to experience heart attacks (Lynch, 1977). Women who had a confiding relationship with a spouse or boyfriend were shown to be less likely to become depressed (Brown & Harris, 1978; Golding, 1989). Both men and women in relationships rated as high in intimacy were less likely to report symptoms of depression and anxiety than those in relationships rated as low in intimacy (Waring, Patton, Neron, & Linker, 1986).

Studies of the relationship between intimacy and depression in women suggest that intimacy is associated with well-being in two ways. First, the availability of an intimate confiding relationship is associated with lower levels of psychological symptoms during periods of stress (Brown & Harris, 1978, 1986; Waltz, Badura, Pfaff, & Schott, 1988). A study that sampled semi-rural mothers reporting a stressful life event found that the rate of affective disorder was lower for those who viewed their husbands as confidants than for those who did not (Solomon & Bromet, 1982).

Second, intimacy seems to provide a buffer even in nonstressful times. Indeed, the availability of an intimate confiding relationship may be the source of the protective effect of marriage reported in Chapter 1. Costello (1982) found that, independent of stressful life events, women who were depressed were twice as likely to lack a confidant as women who were not depressed. Similarly, Hallstrom (1986), studying a large sample of Swedish women, found that independent of the occurrence of any major stress life event, lack of intimacy (operationalized as never married, divorced, widowed, or reporting poor support from husband or deterioration of marriage) increased the risk of depression.

Finally, VanFossen (1981), using a sample of over 1,400 urban, married people from the Midwest, measured the extent to which several relationship characteristics, including partners' perceptions of intimacy and affirmation, predicted depression levels. Intimacy was measured by three items: (a) "My husband/wife is someone I can really talk with about things that are important to me"; (b) "My husband/wife is someone who is a good sexual partner"; and (c) "My husband/wife is someone who is affectionate towards me." Affirmation was measured by three items similar to the validation components of intimacy: (a) "My husband/wife seems to bring out the best qualities in me"; (b) "My husband/wife appreciates me just as I am"; (c) "My marriage . . . gives me . . . (the) opportunity to become the sort of person I'd like to be."[2] Depression was assessed by respondents' indication of the frequency with which they had experienced each of six symptoms in the preceding week: lack of enthusiasm for doing anything, a poor appetite, feeling lonely, feeling bored or having little interest in doing things, having trouble getting to sleep or staying asleep, and feeling downhearted or blue.

Affirmation was very important to the emotional well-being of both husbands and wives. Intimacy and affirmation were especially important for husbands and unemployed wives; whereas perceptions of affirmation and reciprocity were particularly important for employed wives. According to VanFossen (1986), having someone who is a confidant and who appreciates that one is important not only softens the effects of deleterious stresses and strains in life but also contributes in a direct and independent way to emotional well-being.

✎ Gender Differences in Intimacy

More men than women (by 8% to 9%) in VanFossen's (1981) study indicated that they received affirmation and intimacy from their spouse. Other studies have shown similar findings. White married undergraduates were asked to focus on the person closest to them (excluding parents and siblings). Although the majority of husbands and wives described their relationship with their spouse, wives were twice as likely as husbands (22% vs. 12%) to describe a relationship with a same-sex best friend rather than with their husband (Fischer & Narus, 1981).

Among the married, both men and women said that their "other," or cross-sex, relationship should be the most intimate. Yet contrary to what they thought should be, more women than men said that it was easier to talk with those of their own sex (Reisman, 1990). Indeed, 64% of a sample of married heterosexual women reported being more emotionally intimate with other women, compared to only 11% who said they were more emotionally intimate with men (Rosenbluth, in press). Wives are less likely than their husbands to talk about their worries with only their spouse (Veroff, Douvan, & Kulka, 1981), and men are more likely than women to name their spouse as their best friend, most trusted confidant, or the one to whom they would most likely turn in emotional distress (Rubin, 1983).

Studies of African Americans show a similar pattern. Among married black women, 43% named a family member (exclusive of spouse) as the person "to whom they felt closest," 33.3% named a female friend, and only 19.6% named their spouse. When asked to whom they would turn *first* for help with an emotional problem, such as feeling depressed, nervous, or anxious, the majority cited family members or professionals (physicians, ministers, or psychologists) and only one third said they would first seek support from their husbands (Brown & Gary, 1985). A probability sample comparing the responses of black and white husbands and wives found that, of the four groups, white husbands felt best, and black wives felt worst, about the ways in which they and their spouses "confided in each other (and) talked things over" (Scanzoni, 1975). Findings such as these have led some to suggest that women's intimacy needs are not met as completely by their spouses as are men's, and, as a result, women are more likely than men to maintain their same-sex friendships after marriage to assure that their intimacy needs are met (Tschann, 1988).

Studies of Friendship

Studies of friendship patterns show that men report receiving more acceptance, nurturance, and intimacy in their cross-sex friendships than do women (Rose, 1985; Sapadin, 1988). Men are more than twice as likely as women to say they derive more therapeutic value from cross-sex than same-sex friendships (Aukett, Ritchie, & Mill, 1988), and men also report that they self-disclose more and get more enjoyment and feelings of happiness from their cross-sex than same-sex friends.

The reverse is true for women. Women tend to self-disclose more, feel happy more often, and derive more enjoyment from their relationships with other women (Helgeson et al., 1987; Sapadin, 1988). Helgeson et al. described men's and women's experiences of intimacy as more similar than different, but just different enough to cause misunderstandings. The question here is, are the differences also just enough to be a factor in the differential well-being of husbands and wives?

When male and female college students were asked about the types of friendships they wanted, most (82% of the women and 73% of the men) said they would prefer a few intimate friends with whom they could really communicate and confide feelings and problems, over many good but less intimate friends. No gender differences were found in the total number of friends or in the number of intimate, good, or casual friends these students had. Yet despite similarities in professed preferences, similarities in access, and similarities in how the sexes define an intimate friend, men's interactions are generally perceived as less personal, less disclosing, and less intimate than women's (Caldwell & Peplau, 1982).

Men typically get together with more friends than do women and share activities and talk that is centered around work, sports, or expertise (Caldwell & Peplau, 1982; Rubin, 1983; Sapadin, 1988). When males disclose, much of what they say is factual and neutral or positive in emotional tone (Brehm, 1992). Women more often meet their best friend just to talk, sharing intimacies, self-revelation, nurturance, and emotional support (Reisman, 1990). Compared to men, women disclose more personal and feeling-oriented material and are more willing to share emotions that are negative. Overall, the literature suggests that female dyads are usually highest in intimacy, mixed dyads next highest, and male dyads lowest (Fischer & Narus, 1981).

✦ Why a Gender Difference in Intimate Behavior?

Reis, Senchak, and Solomon (1985) assessed several possible explanations for the differences in men's and women's intimate relating. Among the questions they asked were, do men and women evaluate the level of intimacy in the same interaction differently? Are men less likely than women to label interactions as intimate? Are men simply less capable of intimate interactions? To all these questions they answered no. Gender differences in intimate relating have been described as neither "inherent nor immutable" (Sapadin, 1988) but primarily a matter of preference. Others have argued that there is no evidence of a difference in capacity for intimate relating, yet there is some evidence that men tend to respond to conversations about highly intimate topics by withdrawing, whereas women tend to respond by approaching. Similarly, McAdams and his colleagues found that men and women do not differ on measures of fear of intimacy, but women show greater intimacy motivation (McAdams, Lester, Brand, McNamara, & Lensky, 1988).

Men's tendency to relate less intimately has been explained both in terms of social norms (Lewis, 1978) and family organizational patterns (Chodorow, 1978). In the vast majority of families, men and women do not share parenting equally. Women continue to be the primary caretakers and primary attachment figures, which creates different developmental tasks for boys and girls. To identify with a same-sex parent, boys must separate themselves from their primary identification with their mothers, whereas girls do not. To achieve this shift, boys often reject all things feminine, including the feminine or nurturing parts of themselves. As a result of this process, boys are thought to grow up with more rigid ego boundaries and a stronger need for separation, autonomy, and individuation than do girls. For all of us, the tension between separation and relatedness, autonomy and attachment, is a "fundamental dialectic throughout the lifespan" (Wynne & Wynne, 1986, p. 391). Yet there may be a gender skew in the dialectic. As a result of our family organizational patterns, men are forced to separate at an early age and subsequently struggle with issues of nurturance and relatedness; women are more likely to remain related but subsequently struggle with issues of separation and individuation.

From the social norms perspective, intimacy, particularly as it involves disclosure, self-revelation, and emotional vulnerability, is inconsistent with the traditional male role. Self-revelation and emotional vulnerability are viewed as liabilities in competitive contexts, and this has led some to wonder whether women's relationships will change as a function of their increased participation in the paid labor force. To date, studies of professional women show little change. Among a sample of men and women working in banking, law, medicine, publishing, and government service, same-sex friendships were rated higher in overall quality by women than by men, and women reported feeling more nurtured by their female than their male friends in both personal and career areas (Sapadin, 1988). Similarly, a meta-analysis of 205 studies found no changes in gender differences in disclosure patterns over 30 years of research (Dindia & Allen, 1992). According to Sapadin, "gender differences in same and cross-sex friendships remain strong despite new career roles for women" (p. 387). Other normative explanations of gender differences in intimate relating include the lack of emotionally expressive male role models and the pressures against male same-sex intimacy emanating from societal fears and censure of male homosexuality.

Whatever the source, gender differences in intimate relating have a noticeable effect on relationships, and men, more than women, may be the intimacy delimiters. A study examining the predictors of intimacy in lesbian and heterosexual relationships found that women's personality characteristics, including self-esteem and capacity for intimacy, were strongly associated with relationship intimacy for women in same-sex couples but were unrelated to relationship intimacy for women in cross-sex couples

(Rosenbluth & Steil, 1995). One would certainly expect both self-esteem and capacity for intimacy to correlate with achieved intimacy. Why, then, was this the case for women in lesbian but not heterosexual relationships?

The women in same-sex couples were 5 years older, had older partners, and earned more money than the women in cross-sex relationships. In all other respects, the women were virtually indistinguishable; there were no differences in self-esteem, capacity for intimacy, or years of cohabitation. All had been living with the same spouse or romantic partner for an average of 5 years, but no fewer than 2 and no more than 10 years. Seventy-three percent of the women in cross-sex couples were married; 86% of the women in lesbian couples considered themselves married. None had children living at home. Both groups rated their relationships as highly intimate.

The most salient and consistent difference between the two groups, then, was not in the characteristics of the women themselves but in the extent to which these characteristics were associated with the quality of their relationships. Because husbands were not participants in the study, we cannot know with certainty what caused the differences. As we have seen, however, the literature suggests that men are less motivated toward intimate interactions. Because intimacy, by definition, is mutual and reciprocal, it seems reasonable to speculate that the partner who prefers more distance and less interaction will determine the level of intimacy a couple can achieve.

Consistent with this interpretation of the findings, other studies have shown that husbands' communication skills, but not wives'; husbands' relationship talk, but not wives'; and husbands' intimacy maturity, but not wives', discriminate between couples who are high and low in marital adjustment (as assessed by measures of relationship satisfaction, closeness, expressions of affection, and lack of destructive conflict; Acitelli, 1992; Gottman & Potterfield, 1981; Noller, 1980; White, Speisman, Jackson, Bartis, & Costos, 1986).

Differences between lesbian and heterosexual couples might also be explained by differences in level of relationship equality. One of the legacies of traditional gender roles is that men continue to have more power in relationships than do women. Lesbian relationships, in contrast, have been shown to be less dominated by gender-role expectations and behavior (Blumstein & Schwartz, 1983). Based on a "best friends" rather than a "husband-wife" model, lesbian couples develop patterns of interaction based on the unique characteristics of each partner (Bell & Weinberg, 1978) and are widely considered to be more equal. When women are the low-power partners, their personal capacities and personalities are less likely to have an effect because the more powerful partner, like the more distancing partner, is likely to set the relational limits.

ᵉᵃ Emotion Work

Fishman (1978), in a detailed analysis of the conversations of white professional couples at home, illustrated the ways in which husbands disproportionately determine the level of intimate relating. An analysis of 52 hours of taped conversations showed that wives were three times more likely than their husbands to ask questions as a means of initiating and maintaining interaction. Wives used minimal responses, such as "yeah" and "umm" during pauses, to demonstrate interest in both the interaction and the speaker. Husbands, however, were more likely to use these same minimal responses to display a *lack* of interest.

Wives tried more often to initiate conversation and succeeded less often. Husbands tried less often but seldom failed. Wives' failures were due to the failure of husbands to respond. Husbands succeeded more often because wives did the interactional work. Thus, according to Fishman (1978), the definition of what was appropriate or inappropriate conversation became the husbands' choice.

Although the intimacy literature highlights gender differences in *experienced* intimacy, studies such as Fishman's highlight the gender differences in the *work* of intimacy. Societal myths encourage a view of intimacy as something that develops naturally and that women are naturally good at. Such constructions, however, mask the fact that successful interaction does not just happen but is dependent on the work of the participants. Such work, often called emotion work, often goes unacknowledged. Emotion work involves the efforts partners make to understand each other, to empathize with the other's situation, and to make a partner's feelings part of one's own (England & Farkas, 1986).

Other studies have asked men and women what is most important to them in relationships and who contributes what. Of 144 elements, three of the top six items rated as most important by men and women alike related to interaction or emotion work: being committed to the relationship, being sociable and pleasant to be with, and being attentive. Both men and women reported that women contributed far more in each of these areas than did their partners (VanYperen & Buunk, 1990). Women have also reported that they are more likely than their partners to commit themselves to the other person and to the future of the relationship, to remember special occasions, to be thoughtful about sentimental things, and to show affection (Kidder et al., 1981). Societal constructions that view these nurturing, comforting, and facilitating activities as part of women's natural feminine proclivities obscure the fact that these activities require time, energy, effort, and skill. Rather than being perceived as work that women do, they are seen as part of what a woman "is." This results in a failure to recognize these activities as another aspect of family work, such as housekeeping and child care, that women disproportionately perform (Erickson, 1993). Both women and men view these activities as women's spontaneously offered expressions of love. Men, for whom such work is seen as less natural, are free to provide less but are disproportionately appreciated for what they do.

❧ Summary and Conclusions

What can we conclude? First, intimacy is interpersonal, reciprocal, and validating. Intimacy is a process that develops, fluctuates, and changes over time and is never completed or fully accomplished. Intimate relationships require mutual commitment to the other and to the relationship. They take time to develop and effort to maintain. Because mutuality and validation are fundamental to the achievement of intimacy, a number of scholars, as we saw in Chapter 4, state that mature intimacy can develop only in a context of equality (McAdams, 1988; Rubin, 1983).

Availability and quality of intimacy seem to be associated with well-being for men and women alike. Yet for both men and women, it seems that many of their intimacy needs are met primarily by women. Friendship studies show that female dyads are highest in intimacy, cross-sex dyads are next highest, and male dyads are lowest. Studies of marital couples show that though the majority of husbands and wives list their spouses as the person closest to them, wives are less likely to do so than are husbands. Similarly, husbands are more likely than wives to name their spouse as their best friend, most trusted confidant, or the one to whom they would most likely turn to in emotional distress. Returning to the perspective of the "his" and "hers" marriage, then, "his" is more intimate than "hers." Wives' marriages are less affirming, less validating, and less nurturing than their husbands'.

Most investigators see the gender differences in intimate relating as a matter of preference and motivation rather than capacity. Husbands, overall, seem to want lower levels of intimate engagement than wives and generally have more power in heterosexual relationships. Husbands do less of the emotional and interactional work that intimacy requires, and husbands, more often than wives, set the intimacy limits in their relationships. Husbands, then, seem to set the intimacy limits at a lower level than their wives desire while simultaneously receiving more intimacy support than they provide.

The consequences of this asymmetry are costly for both partners.[3] The literature consistently shows that wives are less satisfied with their marriages than are husbands. Wives are also twice as likely as husbands to be depressed. Many have suggested that the differences in well-being are at least partially explained by findings that show that wives provide better emotional support for their husbands' problems than husbands provide for their wives' problems (Veroff, Douvan, & Kulka, 1981).

Although the disruption of relationships, whether through divorce or death, is painful for all, there is evidence of gender asymmetry here as well. Studies of divorce suggest that husbands disproportionately suffer from the loss of emotional support whereas women suffer from the loss of economic support (Brehm, 1992). Consistent with this view, divorced husbands are more likely to remarry, and remarry sooner, than are their spouses (Norton & Moorman, 1987). Studies have shown that men who lose their wives are not only more depressed than their married counterparts but are also more depressed than women of any marital status. This was not the case for widowed women, who were not only less depressed than widowed men but were also less depressed than their married counterparts (Aneshensel et al., 1981; Stroebe & Stroebe, 1983). Thus, the gendered asymmetries in intimacy *work* and intimacy *reception* are detrimental to both partners. They undermine the well-being benefits of marriage for women and leave husbands disproportionately dependent on their wives to have their intimacy needs met.

❧ Notes

1. Others have called attention to the costs and benefits of social support. Belle (1982), in particular, focused on the costs of extended networks when one is called on to provide more support to others than one receives in return. This seems particularly relevant to low-income mothers, who often face high demands combined with lower choice about whether they will enter into or maintain particular relationships. These mothers, according to Belle, are least "free from drain" in their own lives and often have to band together for their own survival and that of their children.

2. VanFossen's (1981) study is conceptualized as a study of social support rather than of intimacy per se. Social support is usually construed as being comprised of instrumental, informational, and emotional assistance. Of these, emotional support is generally viewed as most important to well-being (Thoits, 1985). Studies of social support usually include investigations of extended networks reaching beyond one's spouse. As VanFossen's measures were consistent with those from the intimacy literature and focused exclusively on spouses, it seemed appropriate for inclusion here.

3. One might argue that women do not suffer so much from the asymmetry in intimacy between husbands and wives because wives make up the difference through their female friendships. Consistent with this position, Prager (1995) reports that couples who maintain high levels of intimacy with friends appear to have more satisfying relationships, perhaps because friends fulfill intimacy needs when marital relationships do not. Prager suggests that the intimacy of their friendships might allow spouses who would otherwise experience loneliness if they

had to rely solely on their marriages to feel satisfied. This position, however, fails to address the issue of the costs of unfulfilled expectations. Most women probably do not enter into marriage with the expectation that the work of intimacy will be nonreciprocal and that they will rely on their same-sex friendships to compensate for relational deficits (see also Kelley & Burgoon, 1991).

6

"His" and "Her" Marriage of the '90s

Why Is Relationship Equality So Difficult to Achieve?

I have been supportive of my wife since the beginning of time, and she has been supportive of me. It's not sacrifice; it's family.

Martin Ginsburg, husband of Ruth Bader Ginsburg, at the time of her appointment to the Supreme Court (Labaton, 1993, p. 1)

Women have convinced ourselves that we can do what men can do. But we haven't convinced ourselves, and therefore we haven't convinced our country, that men can do what women can do.

Gloria Steinem, addressing the 1995 annual meeting of the American Psychological Association (DeAngelis, 1955, p. 6)

S ince the 1970s, when Jesse Bernard first published *The Future of Marriage,* the demographics of American families have changed considerably. Many of the demographic changes have been paralleled by attitudinal and behavioral changes. Yet although much has changed, much also remains the same. In some realms, attitudinal changes have not kept pace with the changing demographics, whereas in others, changes in behavior have not kept pace with changing attitudes.

⮞ From the 1970s to the 1990s: Demographic Changes

Choosing to Marry

Over 90% of the population still marries, but the racial gap in the likelihood of ever marrying has widened dramatically. In 1970, 93.4% of all men and 94.5% of all women had been married at some time. By 1991, the percentage of ever-married men had risen slightly to 96.3%, whereas the percentage of ever-married women decreased somewhat to 92.5%. The decline in the likelihood of women's ever marrying is primarily due to the decreased likelihood of marriage for minority women. In 1990, 96.1% of white women had been married at some time by the age of 54, compared to 91.9% of black women and 91.8% of Hispanics.

Looking at the rising racial differences in marriage rates from the perspective of the *currently,* compared to the *ever,* married, Table 6.1 shows that in 1970, over three fourths of white men, 74% of Hispanic, and 67% of black males age 18 and over were currently married. But in 1994, approximately 65% of white men and 56% of Hispanic men age 18 or over were currently married, compared to only 46% of black men. And by 1994, black women were less likely to be currently married than any other group. Only 40% of black women were married, compared to almost 61% of white and Hispanic women.

Those who do marry are waiting longer to do so. In 1970, the median age of women and men at the time of their first marriage was 20.6 and 22.5 years, respectively. By 1994, the estimated me-

Table 6.1 Marital Status by Sex, Race, and Hispanic Origin of Persons Age 18 and Over for the Years 1970 and 1994

	Male		Female	
	1970	*1994*	*1970*	*1994*
White				
Never married	18.2	24.9	13.2	17.1
Married	76.3	64.6	69.3	61.4
Divorced	2.4	8.0	3.8	10.1
Black				
Never married	24.3	42.4	17.4	36.2
Married	66.9	45.9	61.7	40.4
Divorced	3.6	8.7	5.0	12.4
Hispanic				
Never married	21.2	35.4	16.2	24.2
Married	73.8	56.4	70.0	60.2
Divorced	2.7	6.2	5.1	8.7

SOURCE: U.S. Bureau of the Census (1995b), No. 58.

dian age at first marriage had increased to 24.5 and 26.7 years (U. S. Bureau of the Census, 1995a).

Since the mid-1970s, almost one out of every two marriages has ended in divorce. Three fourths of the divorced eventually remarry, usually within 3 years. Men, however, are three times more likely to remarry than are women.

Family Structure

In 1970, 81% of households were families, defined by the U.S. Census as adults or children related by blood, marriage, or adoption. The percentage of the population residing in family households fell to 71% in 1990 and remained the same in 1994 (see Table 6.2). Of those residing in family households, married couples represented slightly more than half (55%) of the population, married couples with children under age 18 just over a quarter of

Table 6.2 Percentage Distribution of Household Types, 1994

Family[a] households	71%
Married couples	55%
With own children under age 18	26%
Without own children under age 18	29%
Male householders, no spouse present	3%
Female householders, no spouse present	13%
Non-family households[b]	29%
Living alone	24%

SOURCE: U.S. Bureau of the Census (1995b), No. 66.
a. A family household is defined by the Census Bureau as a group of two or more persons related by birth, marriage, or adoption who are residing together.
b. Non-family households are those in which one householder lives alone or with unrelated persons.

the population (26%), and single-parent (mostly female-headed) households 13% of the population.

In 1970, 85.2% of all children under the age of 18 were living in a two-parent family. By 1994, the percentage of children living in a two-parent family had declined to 69%, with considerable variability across racial groups. Seventy-six percent of white children, 63% of Hispanic children, but only 33% of black children under the age of 18 were living in two-parent families.

As shown in Table 6.3, over half of black children in 1994 lived in a single-parent, female-headed household; 30% with mothers who had never married. The changing demographics have been costly for children, particularly African American children. In 1993, the median income of married couple households was $43,129, compared with $18,545 for households maintained by women with no husband present. In 1995, 17% of all white children were in poverty, compared to 39% of Hispanic children and 46% of black children (U.S. Bureau of the Census, 1995b).

Paid Employment

In 1970, 59% of all married women with husbands present and almost 70% of those with children under 6 were unemployed. By 1994, these figures were reversed. As shown in Table 6.4, over 60%

(text continues on p. 96)

Table 6.3 Percentage of Children Under 18 Years Old by Presence of Parents and Race for the Years 1970 and 1994

| | Both Parents | Mother Only | | | | Father Only | Neither Parent |
		Divorced	Married/Spouse Absent	Never Married	Widowed		
All Races							
1970	85	3	5	1	2	1	3
1994	69	8	6	9	1	3	4
White							
1970	90	3	3	Z^a	2	1	2
1994	76	8	4	4	1	3	3
Black							
1970	59	5	16	4	4	2	10
1994	33	10	12	30	1	4	10
Hispanic							
1970	78	NA	NA	NA	NA	NA	NA
1994	63	6	9	11	2	4	5

SOURCE: U.S. Bureau of the Census (1995b), No. 79.

a. Z = <.5

Table 6.4 Employment Status of Women by Marital Status and Presence and Age of Children for the Years 1970 and 1994

| | | | | With Any Children | | | | | | | | |
| | | | | Total | | | Children 6-17 Only | | | Children Under 6 | | |
In Labor Force	Never Married	Total Married[a]	Other[b]	Never Married	Married	Other	Never Married	Married	Other	Never Married	Married	Other
1970	53	40.8	39.1	NA	39.7	60.7	NA	49.2	66.9	NA	30.3	50.2
1994	65.1	60.6	47.3	56.9	69.0	73.1	67.5	76.0	78.4	52.2	61.7	62.2

SOURCE: U.S. Bureau of the Census (1995b), No. 638.
a. Husband present.
b. Widowed, divorced, or separated.

of married women and almost 62% of mothers with children under 6 and husbands present are now in the paid labor force.

Until the mid-'70s, black women had much higher labor-force participation rates than white women. By 1994, however, white women were just as likely to be employed as black women, with 58.9% of white women, 58.7% of black women, and 52.9% of Hispanic women in the paid labor force. As women's labor-force participation has increased, men's labor-force participation has declined. In 1970, 79.7% of all men were in the civilian paid labor force, compared to 43.3% of all women. In 1994, 75.1% of all men and 58.8% of all women were in the paid civilian labor force.

Although women overall are still more likely to work part-time and to earn less than their male counterparts, women's financial contributions to the family are increasing. By 1992, fewer than half (42%) of white married men and only a third (33%) of married black men served as the family's main breadwinner, defined as bringing in at least 70% of the family income. In 1992, women's median annual earnings were 70.6% of men's, up from 59.7% in 1979. Today, over 30% of white wives and almost 40% of black wives earn 90% or more of what their husbands earn (Blau, 1996).

Young, highly educated women are those most likely to earn almost as much as men, but the earning ratio begins to decline sharply by age 35. The decline is partly a result of workforce discrimination and partly due to the greater career accommodations that women make as a result of the gendered asymmetries in parental responsibilities. Births to women over age 30 now constitute one third of all births. Although the vast majority of these women will continue to work full-time, most will also accommodate their careers in some way to fit their families.

Summary of the Demographic Changes

Since the 1970s, the face of American families has changed significantly. One quarter of the population (the vast majority of whom are widowed women) is living alone. Approximately one third of the nation's children are living in single-parent (mostly female-headed) households.

The overall marriage rate has changed very little. Over 90% of the population still marry at some time in their life, but they are marrying and having children at an older age than in the past. Married couples still represent slightly more than half of the population, but only one quarter of the population is comprised of married couples with children under age 18. Of these couples, approximately one in five consists of a biological mother and a stepfather rather than a biological father.

Finally, over the last quarter of a century there has a been a dramatic change in women's participation in the paid labor force. Today, in the majority of two-parent families, the wife is employed. Indeed, only one in five families now fits the profile of a breadwinner father and a full-time homemaker mother (Coltrane, 1996). What was once considered the "traditional" family is no longer typical. Indeed, some have suggested that there is now no such thing as a "typical" family (Wetzel, 1990).

❧ Why the Racial Difference in Marriage Rates?

One of the most puzzling aspects of the changing demographics is why there are racial differences in the likelihood of ever marrying. Fewer than half of black men and women are currently married. Historic, demographic, and attitudinal explanations have been offered, but none seems fully explanatory. Demographic explanations focus on the greater number of marriageable women than men among blacks, due to the higher levels of mortality and incarceration of black, compared to white, men. Other demographic explanations focus on the greater difficulty that black women have in finding men who meet their criteria for husbands (presented in Chapter 1). Black women adhere to traditional mate selection norms, seeking men who are smarter, stronger, and better educated than they and who are good providers. Indeed, both black women and men place more emphasis than their white counterparts on the importance of economic supports before marrying, and black women are less likely than white women to say they would marry someone who has fewer resources than they do (Bulcroft & Bulcroft, 1993).

Perceived economic adequacy has been shown to be the most consistent predictor of all aspects of marital quality for black women (Clark-Nicolas & Gray-Little, 1991). Yet there are more educated black women than black men; black women have higher occupational status than black men; and although black men have higher incomes than black women, black women are much closer in income to black men than white women are to white men (Secord & Ghee, 1986). Restricted economic opportunities make it difficult for black men to assume the traditional provider-role responsibilities of husbands and fathers (Bulcroft & Bulcroft, 1993; South, 1993; Taylor et al., 1990), and as a result, they are typically not as attractive financial partners as white husbands (Browman, 1993).

Other studies, however, suggest that the low marriage rates among African Americans, relative to their non-black counterparts, are more a function of black men's than black women's reluctance to marry. In a study comparing the extent to which black, white, and Hispanic men and women said they would like to marry, black men wanted least and Hispanic men wanted most to marry. Black men and women expressed less desire to marry than their white counterparts, but the difference between black and white men was twice as great as the difference between black and white women.

Neither educational nor socioeconomic factors explained the racial differences in desire to marry. Black men anticipated greater economic improvements from marriage than white men but expected marriage to have a less positive and more negative effect on their personal friendships and sex life than did white men.

South (1993) suggested that young men have a particularly strong attachment to their peer groups, but because of the low marriage rates among black men, they have few friends who are married. Wives and children are perceived as interfering with peer-group relationships and as being a burden on personal and individual freedom. Consistent with this point of view, studies have shown that for black men, marital satisfaction was best predicted by the extent to which marriage allowed personal growth and individuality (Clark-Nicolas & Gray-Little, 1991).

Finally, both black men and women, but particularly black women, are less likely than whites to feel that their marriages are harmonious and satisfying (Browman, 1993). For black men, employment difficulties and discouragement with the husband and father roles have also been associated with low levels of satisfaction with family life (Bowman, 1990).

❧ From the 1970s to the 1990s: Attitudinal Changes

The changing demographics have, to some extent, been paralleled by changing attitudes. In 1970, more than 70% of women, including married, college-educated women age 35 and under, said that it is more important for a wife to help her husband's career than to have a career herself (Mason et al., 1976). In 1974, half of all women and 48% of men said that the most satisfying lifestyle was a traditional marriage where the husband worked and the wife stayed home and took care of the house and children. In the early 1980s, surveys showed that 50% of Americans believed that "working mothers are bad for children" and "weaken the family as an institution," and that 70% of women and 85% of men believed that maternal employment was in part responsible for the breakdown of family life (Greenberger, Goldberg, Crawford, & Granger, 1988).

By 1990, many of these figures were reversed. For example, a survey of randomly selected adults from across the country found that more than half (57%) of the population said that the ideal marriage was one in which both the husband and the wife had jobs and shared in the responsibilities of child rearing and caring for the home (DeStefano & Colasanto, 1990). A significant minority (37%), however, maintained that the traditional roles of man as provider and women as homemaker were best.

But what do these attitudinal changes really mean? As we saw in Chapter 4, endorsement of wives having jobs is not necessarily an endorsement of wives having equally high-paying jobs of equally high status. Nor is it an endorsement of wives having an equal responsibility to provide for their families financially. Wilkie (1993) distinguished between provider role *enactment*, assessed as approval or disapproval of a married woman's earning money, and provider role *responsibility*, defined as endorsement of a long-term obligation to earn a significant part of essential family income. Twenty-one percent of men rejected women's provider role enactment, saying that among the married, only men should earn money. Consistent with the findings reported in Chapter 4, twice as many men, or 47%, rejected the idea of women having provider responsibility, saying that it is much better for everyone if the man is the achiever outside the home and the woman takes care of the home and family.

Educational level and employment status are the best predictors of women's attitudes. Highly educated women (particularly those with at least some college) and women who are employed full time hold the most egalitarian attitudes (Mason et al., 1976). For men, age, education, income level, marital status, and wives' employment status are all strong attitude predictors. In particular, older, less well-educated, married, and, among the married, men with full-time homemaker wives are less egalitarian in their views than younger, unmarried, highly educated, high-status men with wives employed full-time (Wilkie, 1993).

Black men, in Wilkie's (1993) survey, were the most egalitarian and Hispanic men the least egalitarian. As Wilkie pointed out, however, racial differences in attitudes were paralleled by racial differences in demographics. Black men in the sample tended to be younger, and a higher proportion of them were unmarried. Of the married, more had wives who were employed full-time. Hispanic men in the sample had lower education levels, and a lower proportion of the married had wives who were employed full-time. The causal relationship here between attitudes and behaviors is unclear. Are wives unemployed because they and their husbands prefer that they be full-time homemakers? Or when wives enter the paid labor force, do they and their husbands begin to believe that a marriage in which both partners are employed is best?

As early as 1970, over 55% of women said that "men should share the work around the house with women such as doing dishes, cleaning, and so forth." By 1974, almost 80% of women endorsed this item (Mason et al., 1976). But just as support for women's right to "earn" is different from endorsing women as "providers," an endorsement of husbands "sharing" child rearing or caring for the home is not necessarily an endorsement of husbands having equal responsibility or spending equal time in either realm. Indeed, despite a 20-year endorsement of husbands sharing in the work of the home, only a small minority (somewhere between 2% and 12%) of husbands share this work equally (see Chapter 4).

Conclusions

Many of the attitude questions discussed in this section were taken from national surveys conducted for other purposes. Thus, the questions asked do not always represent the best measure of the concept under discussion. Nor are the questions always asked in exactly the same way from year to year. Despite these limitations, however, it seems clear that attitudes toward women as providers have not kept pace with the realities of wives' actual employment behavior and financial contributions to the family. In contrast, husbands' actual participation in the work of the home has not kept pace with changing attitudes. Across all measures, attitudes have become increasingly egalitarian. Yet as we saw in Chapter 4, equality has yet to be achieved.

❧ Why Is Relationship Equality So Difficult to Achieve?

A complex interaction of individual, cultural, and relationship factors make achieving relationship equality difficult. Before addressing the complexities of the interactions, however, there are several points that I wish to emphasize.

- Relationship equality is inconsistent with, and unachievable within, the context of separate gender roles.

- Relationship equality is generally perceived as something that primarily benefits women and is achieved only at significant cost to men.
- Even among couples who endorse egalitarian ideals, women disproportionately bear the burden of initiating and enforcing change.
- The motivation to seek change requires a perception of inequality as unfair.
- Women are impeded in perceiving inequality to be unfair by gender differences in the sense of entitlement emanating from the ideology of separate gender roles.
- A woman's role as change agent conflicts with her role as nurturer and relationship maintainer.

Relationship equality is inconsistent with, and unachievable within, the context of separate gender roles. The defining dichotomy of the ideology of separate gender roles is that men are responsible for providing financially for their families, whereas women are responsible for providing nurturance and maintaining relationships. In Chapter 4, considerable evidence was presented showing how this ideology undermines men's and women's abilities to achieve equal relationships. Separate gender roles limit wives' access to universally valued resources, ascribe different meanings to the resources that husbands and wives contribute, and prescribe differences in men's and women's sense of entitlement.

An important point to note is that the relationship between an ideology of separate gender roles and gender inequality is not restricted to the United States but extends across widely divergent societies and cultures. In 1992, studies of eight industrialized countries in Europe and Asia showed that the extent to which masculinity is defined by the breadwinner role, women are perceived as working from choice rather than from necessity, and societies endorse the belief that infants need full-time maternal care, are primary factors in determining career opportunities for women and role sharing among couples. When children are believed to require full-time maternal care and mothers allegedly work by choice, there is little societal or partner support for women in the paid labor force. Societies that endorse these beliefs provide little public child care, free husbands from domestic responsibilities, and leave employed mothers to work out their own support systems. According to the authors of these studies, when men are defined as breadwinners and women as homemakers, there is no restructuring of paid or domestic work to take into account women's employment. Thus, for women, equality at work means equality with men under conditions established for men without home responsibility (Lewis, Izraeli, & Hootsmans, 1992).

Coltrane (1996), in a comparative analysis of nonindustrialized societies in Africa, Asia, the Middle East, and the South Pacific, found that societies in which men develop and maintain close relationships with young children are more likely to view men and women as inherently equal. The more that fathers were involved in child care, measured in terms of frequency of father-child proximity (e.g., holding and touching infants), the more routine child care (e.g., feeding) that was performed by men. The more men expressed emotional warmth and support toward children, the less misogynistic men were and the more social and political power women had. In contrast, the more distant the father-child relationships, the more men believed that women were inferior to men and the more women were excluded from public rituals.

Relationship equality is generally perceived as something that primarily benefits women and is achieved only at significant cost to men. In the vast majority of unequal relationships, women are the less benefited partner. Women in unequal relationships suffer from excessive domesticity, restricted opportunities for personal achievement and public participation, and low self-esteem. Reflecting the objective status hierarchy of work, simply being employed reflects some upward mobility for women in terms of increased power, independence, prestige, and self-esteem (Hunt & Hunt, 1987). Thus, gender asymmetries in opportunities for achievement, self-development, and establishing an independent sense of self-worth have led to the view that any movement in the direction of equality primarily benefits women.

For men, who have typically been the partner most benefited, the achievement of gender equality is most often viewed in terms of cost, specifically interference with men's abilities to meet career demands, loss of the power and privileges associated with being the sole provider, loss of the services of an unemployed wife, increased stress, and demands to participate in family life in unfamiliar ways that conflict with masculine identity. Considerably less attention has been paid to the costs of inequality for men, including both excessive careerism (or work involvement) and loss of their nurturing, care-giving selves (Hunt & Hunt, 1987).

The ways in which men benefit from greater relationship equality have been largely neglected. For men, the benefits of relationship equality include relief from the achievement and performance pressures associated with their sole breadwinner role; richer, more intimate, and more satisfying relationships with their wives and children (see Chapters 4 and 5); and greater freedom to authentically express and experience themselves (Hunt & Hunt, 1987).

Improved Intimacy

As shown in Chapter 5, one of the most important aspects of relationships is the level of intimacy that partners achieve. Yet considerable asymmetries exist in the extent to which women and men seek and contribute to the quality of intimate interaction. The most widely accepted explanation of the source of this disparity addresses the different developmental tasks imposed on boys, compared to girls. Because women continue as the primary caretakers, boys and girls initially identify with their mothers. To shift to a male identity, boys must incorporate a male persona and, in doing so, often reject all things feminine. Further, the absence of men from most parenting and nurturing tasks means that the masculinity internalized by little boys is based on distance, separation, and a fantasy image of what constitutes manhood (Kaufman, 1994). The acquisition of masculinity, then, becomes a process through which men come to suppress a range of emotions, needs, and possibilities, such as nurturing, receptivity, and empathy. But these emotions and needs do not disappear. As Kaufman points out, "The strange thing about men's trying to suppress emotions is that it leads not to less but to more emotional dependency" (p. 149).

Consistent with these theories, Silberstein (1992), in a series of in-depth interviews, found that a frequent theme in men's discussions of their relationships with their own parents were feelings of anger, resentment, and deprivation emanating from a loss of attention from their absent fathers. As a result of these concerns, a major theme in the emerging psychology of men is that important benefits will accrue not only to wives and children, but to husbands and relationships, from men's greater involvement in parenting.

In one of the few empirical studies of these issues, Coltrane (1996) interviewed a sample of fathers who shared equally in parenting. Many of these men were fathers in dual-earner families where the parents worked split shifts. As a result, the fathers were forced to overcome feelings of ambivalence and awkwardness and assume the role of primary caretaker in their wives' absence.

According to Coltrane, one of the most common lessons men learned from fathering was how to be attentive. Most described child care as an opportunity to grow and mature and said that being a parent helped them work through unresolved emotional issues with their own fathers. Child care was described as qualitatively different from their interactions with women, free of ambivalence and fear of intimacy. Yet in both this and other studies, as men became more sensitive parents, their marital relations improved as well (Coltrane, 1996; Jump & Haas, 1987). As a result of learning how to care for their children, fathers also paid more attention to emotional cues from their wives and engaged in more reciprocal communication.

Reduced Stress

Equal relationships are widely viewed as more stressful than more traditional relationships. As reported in Chapter 4, the disadvantage of relationship equality most frequently cited by men and women was the negative effect that equality can have on marital relationships by requiring daily negotiations and compromise. Yet, contrary to respondents' own expectations, study findings show exactly the opposite (Steil & Whitcomb, 1992). When the amount of stress reported by men and women in equal, transitional, and traditional relationships was compared, it was found that women and men in egalitarian relationships reported feeling stressed by the responsibilities arising from their marital relationships *least* often, whereas those in traditional relationships reported feeling stressed *most* often.

Although equal relationships require more frequent negotiation and compromise, it may be precisely the need for continued interpersonal contact and involvement that contributes to the high levels of satisfaction found among egalitarian couples (Gray-Little & Burks, 1983; Scanzoni, 1979). In this regard, I quote one of the male respondents in the study described in Chapter 4, who said,

> Maybe you end up having certain arguments that you might not have had, arguments about whose responsibility it is to do this, that, and the other. But I think in a way, if you don't have those arguments, you end up having arguments about other things sooner or later. The arguments you have about responsibilities are not as vicious as the ones you have later about resentment. (Rosenbluth et al., under revision)

Perhaps because equality is viewed as primarily benefiting women, it has been consistently shown that *women disproportionately bear the burden of initiating change*. Even among the sample of dual-career respondents described in Chapter 4, for whom there were no differences in the extent to which the men and women reported equality as important in their own relationships, 90% of wives and 55% of husbands said that the wives were more likely to raise issues of equality in their own relationships (Rosenbluth et al., under revision). Yet women are impeded in their role as change agents by their reluctance to report their relationships as unfair.

The motivation to seek change requires a perception of inequality as unfair. Extensive literature from the psychology of justice suggests that the motivation to seek change requires a perception of unfairness (Steil, 1994). Yet one of the paradoxes of the relationship literature is wives' lack of grievance over the inequalities of their lives at home. Across all domains of domestic life, including responsibilities, nurturance, and opportunities for personal development, the literature shows considerable gender-based imbalance, yet women report little sense of grievance. Crosby (1982) found that employed wives did twice as much work at home as their husbands but were no less satisfied. Berk (1985) reported the findings of a national survey of husbands and wives that asked, "Now thinking about who does what around the house, do you think these arrangements are fair?" and "Thinking in terms of how fair these arrangements are, do you feel you should be doing a lot less housework . . ., a lot more, or the same?" Ninety-four percent of husbands said that the arrangements were somewhat or very fair, 70% of wives said they should be doing "about the same" amount of household work, and an additional 9% of wives said they should be doing more.

Pleck (1985) reported that wives were twice as likely to say they wished their husbands would spend more time in child care than they were to say they wished that husbands would help more with housework. This was not because wives wanted more help for themselves, however, but because they felt that husbands' greater involvement in child care would be beneficial to both father and child.

These findings continue to hold true in the '90s. Wives continue to do at least twice the amount of domestic work as husbands, but the majority of both employed and unemployed wives report the division of labor as fair (Blair & Johnson, 1992; Coltrane, 1996; Hawkins, Marshall, & Meiners, 1995). Hispanic women spend more hours in domestic work and fewer in the paid labor force than non-Hispanic white or black women and are least likely to see the division of household labor as unfair. White men spend fewer hours in domestic work (14.3) than black (17.3) or Hispanic (18.4) men. White and Hispanic men spend more hours in paid employment than black men, but white men were most likely (27% vs. 13% and 19%) to view the division of household work as unfair to their partners (John, Shelton, & Luschen, 1995).

For women, neither their own nor their husbands' hours in paid work, nor husbands' hours in traditionally male domestic tasks, are related to perceptions of fairness. The best predictors of fairness perceptions are the number of hours husbands spend on stereotypically female tasks and the extent to which housework is perceived as appreciated (Blair & Johnson, 1992). Yet husbands' hours spent on female tasks are no more, and are sometimes less, predictive of how the division of labor is perceived than are wives' perceptions that their work is appreciated. Both of these factors together explained only 15% of the variance in women's perceptions of the fairness of work allocations (Blair & Johnson, 1992; Hawkins et al., 1995). Thus, the strongest and most consistent finding is that the majority of employed and unemployed wives report that the unequal distribution of domestic work is fair.

Women are impeded in their perceptions of inequality as unfair by gender differences in the sense of entitlement. As the literature reviewed in Chapter 4 suggested, our sense of entitlement emanates, to a large extent, from socially constructed conceptions of who we are. Who we are, in turn, is often defined in terms of socially constructed roles, including husband compared to wife, provider compared to nurturer, or mother compared to father. Each of these roles carries socially prescribed obligations and rights. But as we also saw in Chapter 4, the combination of rights and obligations has been unequally distributed, and the respective contributions have been unequally valued. The resulting gender differences in the sense of entitlement play a pivotal role in husbands' and wives' perceptions of fairness. Crosby (1982), in a singularly systematic study of the predictors of a sense of injustice, showed that women are unlikely to perceive current conditions as unfair until they see that other conditions are possible, want such conditions for themselves, and believe they are entitled to them.

Most justice researchers view a sense of entitlement as synonymous with a sense of deserving (Major, 1994). But the two constructs are distinct. Whereas a sense of entitlement is based on a conception of inherent rights emanating from who we are, a sense of deserving is based on what we have earned as a result of what we have done. This distinction is important. In Chapter 4, for example, we saw that a high-earning wife may believe, on the basis of her financial contributions to the family, that she deserves

more help at home. However, until this high-earning wife rede-
fines herself as a coprovider, she will not feel entitled to the same
rights as her husband. She will be negotiating for limited goals
(help) on the basis of what she deserves rather than for the larger
goal (equally shared responsibility) to which she is entitled. Moreover, she will be negotiating from a lower-status position. Conversely, a husband may agree that his wife deserves (or maybe
needs) some help. But until fathering is redefined to include a view
of men as conurturers, he will be operating from an entitled, rather
than a deserving, position, and he will not perceive himself as
equally responsible for the day-to-day care of their children.

According to most justice theorists, both the sense of entitlement
and the sense of deserving are confirmed and challenged through
the process of social comparison. The comparisons we make can
be based on what we have achieved or felt entitled to in the past,
or on our expectations and aspirations for the future. Usually,
however, they are based on our comparisons to a similar other. I
am entitled to what others like me are entitled to; I deserve what
others who do what I do deserve.

One dimension of similarity is gender. Indeed, the endorsement
of separate gender roles makes this dimension particularly salient
and results in a general preference for same-sex rather than cross-
sex comparisons. Women compare their relationships, their outcomes, and their lives to those of other women, whom they see as
more similar to themselves than men. Similarly, men are likely to
compare themselves to other men. When thinking about their
contributions to their relationships, their children, and their home,
they are likely to ask whether they do as much as other men do,
not whether they do as much as their wives do.

Although empirical work in this area is sparse, studies have
shown that when women compare their marital relationships with
those of other women, they tend to be satisfied with their marriages and believe they are faring better than most. When they
compare themselves to men, they tend to be less satisfied
(VanYperen & Buunk, 1991). Hochschild (1989) relates the story
of Nancy, an avowed egalitarian: "In the past, Nancy had compared her responsibilities at home, her identity, her life to Evan's
(her husband)" (p. 49) Yet as time went on and Nancy found

herself unable to renegotiate their relationship, she changed her comparison.

> Now to avoid resentment, she seemed to compare herself more to other working mothers. By this standard she was doing great. Nancy also compared herself to single women who had moved further ahead in their careers, but they fit into another mental category. A single woman could move ahead in her career, but a married woman has do a wife's work and a mother's work as well. She did not make this distinction for men. (p. 49)

For women and for men, the perception of inequality as unfair requires a shift in the choice of comparison from a same-sex to a cross-sex other. In addition, women must give more emphasis to the sense of entitlement and men to the sense of deserving. Thus, women must believe they are entitled not to what other tired, employed mothers are entitled but to the same entitlements that their male partners take for granted. Conversely, men must consider not only what they do relative to other men but also what they do relative to their partners.

But, ironically, *women's role as change agent conflicts with their primary role as nurturer and relationship maintainer.* Because women, as nurturers, are oriented toward fulfilling the needs of others and providing the base from which others depart, their sense of self-worth has often been built on activities that can be defined as taking care of and giving to others, rather than through direct and open pursuit of their own goals (Chodorow, 1978; Miller, 1986). Miller suggests that women often feel that attempts to act on their own behalf or to take steps toward their own growth are repudiations of femininity and will be viewed as attacks on men. As we saw in Chapter 4, women endorse and protect their husbands' provider role. Couples will go to great lengths to conceal a high-earning wife's income, and when women earn more than their partners, they often compensate for this assault on their husbands' masculinity by doing more of the work of the home (Hochschild, 1989).

Women are appropriately wary of the potential costs to themselves, their partners, and their relationships when social norms are violated. When husbands resist change, wives often defer. But as Hochschild (1989) suggests, they pay a heavy price—a devaluation of themselves and their daughters as women and the continuation of inequality.

"His" and "Her" Marriage From the 1970s to the 1990s: Summary and Conclusions

In the early 1970s, Jessie Bernard asserted that there are two marriages in every marital union, "his" and "hers," and that his was better than hers. Bernard emphasized the costs that the differences in the his-and-her marriage imposed on women in terms of impaired well-being.

In the years since the publication of Bernard's book, American families have undergone a quiet revolution. The most significant change has been the rapid influx of wives and mothers into the paid labor force. As a result, wives' roles have expanded dramatically. Yet husbands' roles have not. Women continue to perform a disproportionate amount of the emotion work of relationships, child care, and the work of the home, while simultaneously assuming the responsibilities of paid employment. These relationship asymmetries are costly to men and to women alike. Yet so long as women feel their labors are appreciated, the majority do not seem to feel aggrieved. Thus, change has been difficult to achieve, and inequality persists.

Throughout the preceding chapters, I have suggested that the difficulty in achieving change is the result not only of individual but also dyadic, cultural, and sociostructural forces. Relationship asymmetries begin long before marriage. They emerge from deeply rooted motives, conscious and unconscious, and internalized expectations, implicit and explicit, that reflect and reproduce the values of the larger society. In Chapter 1 we saw the extent to which societal values influence the characteristics that women and men seek in their prospective partners. Women seek men who are older, stronger, smarter, and who will be good providers, whereas men are more likely to seek women who are young and beautiful. The extent to which either women or men fully understand the long-term implications of these gendered criteria is unclear.

Throughout the preceding chapters, I have also tried to show that although the roots of inequality are present before marriage, inequality becomes most salient when there are young children at home.

Figure 6.1 outlines the relationship between several sociostructural, dyadic, and individual factors and the endorsement of core beliefs directly relevant to partners' sense of entitlement, choice of comparison other, relationship equality, and perceptions of relationship fairness. The more women and men believe that men but not women have the responsibility to provide; that men's paid employment is more important to their self-esteem and to family well-being than is women's; that women but not men bear the primary responsibility for nurturing the young; that children require full-time maternal care; and that women's employment is harmful to children, the fewer societal supports there will be for mothers and for families when children are young. Indeed, structural problems, such as job inflexibility and the unavailability of child-care facilities, will be defined as a problem for women rather than as a societally imposed problem for families.

College-educated women who are employed full-time are the least likely to agree that women work by permission rather than right and that paid employment detracts from good mothering. But across all racial, ethnic, and employment groups, the more a woman believes that men are responsible for providing and that women are responsible for the home and for children, the more ambivalent she will feel about change. She will experience more difficulty relinquishing her greater influence over the children and the home, and she will report less grievance with marital inequality. Men who believe that providing is exclusively a male responsibility are more likely to believe that women's employment threatens them and harms children. They are more likely to resist change and to feel distressed when their wives are employed.

Endorsing these beliefs results in a lower sense of entitlement for women, an increased tendency for both women and men to compare to same-sex rather than cross-sex others, and an increased likelihood that both women and men will report unequal relationships as fair.

Figure 6.1. Sociostructural, Dyadic, and Individual Factors Related to Entitlement Level, Perceptions of Relationship Fairness, and Individual and Relationship Well-Being

Sociostructural Factors	Cultural Beliefs	Individual and Dyadic Factors				Relationship Variables
		Husband's and wife's endorsements of cultural beliefs	Wife's sense of entitlement	Wife's comparison other	Relationship equality *assessed as participation in:* child care, decision making, domestic tasks, emotion work, and career valuing	Fairness perceptions
Race	**Male provider role**					
African American	*Derivative beliefs that:*					
Hispanic	Men's paid work is more important to the family	H & W high				
White	Paid work is more important to men's than women's self-esteem	H low W high	Low	Referential (same-sex others)	Unequal	Fair
		H high W low	High	Relational (partner, or cross-sex others)	Equal	Unfair
SES	**Female nurturing role**					
Blue-collar	*Derivative beliefs that:*		**Husband's sense of entitlement**	**Husband's comparison other**		
White-collar	Women's paid work is optional or for self-development	H & W high	High	Referential (same-sex others)		
	Paid employment detracts from good mothering	H high W low				
Employment	Children need full-time maternal care	H high W low				
Part-time employment	Home is a symbolic expression of caring for women more than men	H low W high	Low	Relational (partner, or cross-sex others)		
Full-time employment	Relationship equality primarily benefits women	H & W low				
Full-time homemaker						
Hours in paid employment relative to spouse						
H>W						
H=W						
H<W						
Income relative to spouse						
H>W						
H=W						
H<W						
Children						
Yes						
No						
Sex						
Male						
Female						

Sociostructural factors	Responsibility perceptions
Lack of job flexibility	Wife's problem
Lack of child care	Family problem
	Societal problem

Race, sex, SES, and a number of employment variables are all associated with the extent to which husbands and wives endorse gendered beliefs about providing and nurturing. But across all racial, SES, and employment groups, the greater a woman's endorsement of male provider and female nurturing roles, the lower her sense of entitlement. The lower her sense of entitlement, the more likely she is to make same-sex (referential) rather than cross-sex (relational) comparisons, to report an unequal relationship as fair, and to accept sociostructural problems such as job inflexibility and lack of child care as her own. For a man, higher endorsement of gendered beliefs is associated with higher levels of entitlement. The higher a man's sense of entitlement the more likely he is to make same-sex (referential) rather than cross-sex (relational) comparisons and to also report unequal relationships as fair.

Table 6.2. Individual and Relationship Outcomes Associated With Perceptions of Relationship Fairness

Relationship Equality[a]	Fairness Perceptions	Outcomes
Equal	Fair	**Relationship** satisfaction
	Unfair	intimacy anger
Unequal	Fair	**Individual** well-being
	Unfair	assessed as: anxiety depression somaticism

a. Assessed as participation in: child care, decision making, domestic tasks, emotion work, and career valuing

As outlined in Table 6.2, the perception of unequal relationships as fair can be costly for women, for men, and for the relationships they share. Though women, under these conditions, report little sense of grievance, symptoms of dysphoria and anxiety may belie their professed lack of anger. Similarly, while the majority of women report that they are satisfied when relationships are unequal, their relationships are likely to be less intimate.

Women who endorse egalitarian beliefs are likely to have a higher sense of entitlement, are more likely to compare to their spouses, and are more likely to perceive unequal relationships as unfair. The perception of unfairness usually leads to anger and a desire for change.

When change seems unattainable, some women may choose to leave their relationships, whereas others, like Nancy, may try to accommodate themselves to dependency and the loss of opportunity. In the best-case scenario, either partner's desire for change will lead to a mutual renegotiation of the relationship. Men and women together will be forced to make hard choices. How, they must ask, can I simultaneously be fair to myself, fair to my partner, fair to my children, and fair to my employer? Together, perhaps, they may begin to focus on the larger society, examining the kinds of supports that are needed and insisting that their employers must also be fair to them.

The costs should not be minimized but neither should the rewards. In equal relationships, men have the opportunity to relinquish the mantle of total economic responsibility and family dependency, to involve themselves in parenting, and to more fully express their emotional and nurturing selves. Women have the opportunity to develop themselves professionally, develop a sense of self independent of their husband and their children, and achieve economic independence and higher self-esteem (Gilbert & Rachlin, 1987). Finally, men and women together have the opportunity to be part of more intimate relationships based on the mutual reliance and respect that is so important to a satisfying relationship and to both husbands' and wives' well-being.

References

Acitelli, L. K. (1992). Gender differences in relationship awareness and marital satisfaction among young married couples. *Personality and Social Psychology Bulletin, 18,* 102-110.

Acitelli, L. K., & Duck, S. (1987). *Intimacy as the proverbial elephant.* Newbury Park, CA: Sage.

Aida, Y., & Falbo, T. (1991). Relationships between marital satisfaction, resources, and power strategies. *Sex Roles, 24,* 43-56.

Aldous, J. (1969). Wives' employment status and lower-class men as husband-fathers: Support for the Moynihan thesis. *Journal of Marriage and the Family, 31,* 469-476.

Amaro, H., Russo, N. F., & Johnson, J. (1987). Family and work predictors of psychological well-being among Hispanic women professionals. *Psychology of Women Quarterly, 11,* 505-521.

Amenson, C. S., & Lewinsohn, P. M. (1981). An investigation into the observed sex difference in prevalence of unipolar depression. *Journal of Abnormal Psychology, 90,* 1-13.

Aneshensel, C. S., Frerichs, R. R., & Clark, V. A. (1981). Family roles and sex differences in depression. *Journal of Health and Social Behavior, 22,* 379-393.

Aukett, R., Ritchie, J., & Mill, K. (1988). Gender differences in friendship patterns. *Sex Roles, 19,* 57-66.

Bachrach, L. (1975). *Marital status and mental disorder: An analytic review* (Report of the National Institute of Mental Health). Washington, DC: Government Printing Office.

Bannester, E. M. (1969). Sociodynamics: An integrative theorem of power, authority, influence and love. *American Sociological Review, 34,* 374-393.

Barling, J., & Barenbrug, A. (1984). Some personal consequences of "flexitime" work schedules. *Journal of Social Psychology, 123,* 137-138.

Barnett, R. C., & Baruch, G. K. (1987). Determinants of fathers' participation in family work. *Journal of Marriage and the Family, 49,* 29-40.

Barnett, R. C., & Baruch, G. K. (1985). Women's involvement in multiple roles and psychological distress. *Journal of Personality and Social Psychology, 49,* 135-145.

Baruch, G. K., & Barnett, R. C. (1986). Consequences of fathers' participation in family work: Parents' role strain and well-being. *Journal of Personality and Social Psychology, 51,* 983-992.

Baruch, G. K., Biener, L., & Barnett, R. C. (1987). Women and gender in research on work and family stress. *American Psychologist, 42,* 130-136.

Bebbington, P. (1987). Marital status and depression: A study of English national admission statistics. *Acta Psychiatrica Scandinavica, 75,* 640-650.

Beckett, J. O., & Smith, A. D. (1981). Work and family roles: Egalitarian marriage in black and white families. *Social Service Review, 55,* 314-326.

Bell, A., & Weinberg, M. (1978). *Homosexualities: A study of diversity among men and women.* New York: Simon & Schuster.

Belle, D. (1982). Social ties and social support. In D. Belle (Ed.), *Lives in stress* (pp. 133-144). Beverly Hills, CA: Sage.

Benjamin, J. (1988). *The bonds of love.* New York: Pantheon.

Berheide, C. W. (1984). Women's work in the home: Seems like old times. *Marriage and Family Review, 7*(3-4), 37-55.

Berk, S. (1985). *The gender factory.* New York: Plenum.

Bernard, J. (1981). The good provider role: Its rise and fall. *American Psychologist, 36,* 1-12.

Bernard, J. (1982). *The future of marriage.* (2nd ed.). New Haven, CT: Yale University Press.

Biernat, M., & Wortman, C. B. (1991). Sharing of home responsibilities between professionally employed women and their husbands. *Journal of Personality and Social Psychology, 60,* 844-860.

Bird, C., & Ross, C. (1993). Houseworkers and paid workers: Qualities of the work and effects on personal control. *Journal of Marriage and the Family, 55,* 913-925.

Blair, S., & Johnson, M. (1992). Wives' perceptions of the fairness of the division of household labor: The intersection of housework and ideology. *Journal of Marriage and the Family, 54,* 570-581.

Blau, F. D. (1996). *The economic well-being of American women, 1970-1990.* Unpublished manuscript.

Blood, R. O., & Wolfe, D. M. (1960). *Husbands and wives: The dynamics of married living.* New York: Free Press.

Blumstein, P., & Schwartz, P. (1983). *American couples: Money, work, sex.* New York: William Morrow.

Bowman, P. (1990). Coping with provider role strain: Adaptive cultural resources among Black husband-fathers. *Journal of Black Psychology, 16*(2), 1-21.

Brehm, S. (1992). *Intimate relationships* (2nd ed.). New York: McGraw-Hill.

Browman, C. L. (1991). Gender, work-family roles, and psychological well-being of blacks. *Journal of Marriage and the Family, 53,* 509-520.

Browman, C. L. (1993). Race differences in marital well-being. *Journal of Marriage and the Family, 55,* 724-732.

Brown, D. R., & Gary, L. E. (1985). Social support network differentials among married and nonmarried black females. *Psychology of Women Quarterly, 9,* 229-241.

Brown, G. W., & Harris, T. O. (1978). *Social origins of depression: A study of psychiatric disorder in women.* London: Tavistock.

Brown, G. W., & Harris, T. O. (1986). Stressor, vulnerability and depression: A question of replication. *Psychological Medicine, 16,* 739-744.

Browne, A., & Williams, K. R. (1989). Exploring the effect of resource availability and the likelihood of female-perpetrated homicides. *Law and Society Review, 23*(1), 75-94.

Bryson, S. E., & Pilon, D. J. (1984). Sex differences in depression and the method of administering the Beck Depression Inventory. *Journal of Clinical Psychology, 40,* 529-534.

Bulcroft, R., & Bulcroft, K. (1993). Race differences in attitudinal and motivational factors in the decision to marry. *Journal of Marriage and the Family, 55,* 338-355.

Burke, R., & Weir, J. (1976). Relationships of wives' employment status to husband, wife and pair satisfaction and performance. *Journal of Marriage and the Family, 38,* 279-287.

Burris, B. (1991). Employed mothers: The impact of class and marital status in the prioritization of family and work. *Social Science Quarterly, 72,* 50-66.

Buss, D. (1994). *The evolution of desire.* New York: Basic Books.

Caldwell, M. A., & Peplau, L. A. (1982). Sex differences in same-sex friendship. *Sex Roles, 8,* 721-732.

Campbell, A., Converse, P. E., & Rogers, W. L. (1976). *Quality of American life survey.* New York: Russell Sage Foundation.

Carmen, E., Russo, N. F., & Miller, J. B. (1981). Inequality and women's mental health: An overview. *American Journal of Psychiatry, 138,* 1319-1330.

Cate, R., Lloyd, S., & Henton, J. (1985). The effect of equity, equality and reward level on the stability of students' premarital relationships. *Journal of Social Psychology, 125,* 715-721.

Cate, R., Lloyd, S., Henton, J., & Larson, J. (1982). Fairness and reward level as predictors of relationship satisfaction. *Social Psychology Quarterly, 45,* 177-181.

Chodorow, N. (1978). *The reproduction of mothering: Psychoanalysis and the sociology of gender.* Berkeley: University of California Press.

Clark-Nicolas, P., & Gray-Little, B. (1991). Effect of economic resources on marital quality in Black married couples. *Journal of Marriage and the Family, 53,* 645-655.

Cleary, P., & Mechanic, D. (1983). Sex differences in psychological distress among married people. *Journal of Health and Social Behavior, 24,* 111-121.

Coleman, L. M., Antonucci, T. C., Adelmann, P. K., & Crohan, S. E. (1987). Social roles in the lives of middle-aged and older black women. *Journal of Marriage and the Family, 49,* 761-771.

Coltrane, S. (1996). *Family man: Fatherhood, housework, and gender equality.* New York: Oxford University Press.

Costello, C. G. (1982). Social factors associated with depression: A retrospective community study. *Psychological Medicine, 12,* 329-339.

Crosby, F. J. (1991). *Juggling: The unexpected advantages of balancing career and home for women and their families.* New York: Free Press.

Crosby, F. J. (1982). *Relative deprivation and working women.* New York: Oxford University Press.

D'Arcy, C., & Siddique, C. M. (1985). Marital status and psychological well-being: A cross-national comparative analysis. *International Journal of Comparative Sociology, 26*(3-4), 149-166.

DeAngelis, T. (1995, October). Subtle sexism exists, says keynoter Steinem [Newsline]. *APA Monitor,* p. 6.

Degler, C. N. (1980). *At odds: Women and the family in America from the revolution to the present.* New York: Oxford University Press.

Derogatis, L., Lipman, R., Rickels, K., Uhlenhuth, E., & Coti, L. (1974). The Hopkins Symptom Checklist (HSCL): A self report symptom inventory. *Behavioral Science, 19,* 1-13.

DeStefano, L., & Colasanto, D. (1990). The gender gap in America: Unlike 1975, today most Americans think men have it better. *Gallup Poll News Service, 54*(37), 1-7.

Deutsch, M. (1985). *Distributive justice: A social psychological perspective.* New Haven, CT: Yale University Press.

Dindia, K., & Allen, M. (1992). Sex differences in self-disclosure: A meta-analysis. *Psychological Bulletin, 112,* 106-124.

Dohrenwend, D., & Dohrenwend, B. (1976). Sex differences in psychiatric disorders. *American Journal of Sociology, 81,* 1447-1459.

Dugger, K. (1988). Social location and gender role attitudes: A comparison of Black and White women. *Gender & Society, 2,* 425-448.

Elman, M. R., & Gilbert, L. A. (1984). Coping strategies for role conflict in married professional women with children. *Family Relations, 33,* 431-441.

England, P., & Farkas, G. (1986). *Households, employment, and gender: A social, economic, and demographic view.* New York: Aldine de Gruyter.

Ericksen, J. A., Yancey, W. L., & Ericksen, E. P. (1979). The division of family roles. *Journal of Marriage and the Family, 4,* 301-313.

Erickson, R. (1993). Reconceptualizing family work: The effects of emotion work on perceptions of marital quality. *Journal of Marriage and the Family, 55,* 888-900.

Esterling, B. A., Antoni, M. H., Fletcher, M. A., Margulies, S., & Schneiderman, N. (1994). Emotional disclosure through writing or speaking modulates latent Epstein-Barr virus antibody titers. *Journal of Consulting and Clinical Psychology, 62,* 130-140.

Falbo, T. (1977). Multidimensional scaling of power strategies. *Journal of Personality and Social Psychology, 35,* 537-547.

Falbo, T., & Peplau, L. (1980). Power strategies in intimate relationships. *Journal of Personality and Social Psychology, 38,* 618-628.

Ferree, M. M. (1976). Working class jobs: Housework and paid work as sources of satisfaction. *Social Problems, 22,* 431-441.

Ferree, M. M. (1991). The gender division of labor in two-earner marriages. *Journal of Family Issues, 12,* 158-180.

Fischer, J. L., & Narus, L. R. (1981). Sex roles and intimacy in same sex and other sex relationships. *Psychology of Women Quarterly, 5,* 444-455.

Fishman, P. (1978). Interaction: The work women do. *Social Problems, 25,* 397-406.

Foa, E. B., & Foa, U. G. (1980). Resource theory: Interpersonal behaviors as exchange. In K. J. Gergen, M. S. Greenberg, & R. H. Willis (Eds.), *Social exchange: Advances in theory and research* (pp. 77-94). New York: Plenum.

Fox, J. W. (1980). Gove's specific sex-role theory of mental illness: A research note. *Journal of Health and Social Behavior, 21,* 260-267.

French, J. R., & Raven, B. (1959). The basis for social power. In D. Cartwright (Ed.), *Studies in social power* (pp. 150-167). Ann Arbor, MI: Institute for Social Research.

Fromm, E. (1956). *The art of loving.* New York: Harper.

Genero, N. P., Miller, J. B., Surrey, J., & Baldwin, L. M. (1992). Measuring perceived mutuality in close relationships: Validation of the Mutual

Psychological Development Questionnaire. *Journal of Family Psychology, 6*, 36-48.

Gilbert, L. A. (1985). *Men in dual career families: Current realities and future prospects.* Hillsdale, NJ: Lawrence Erlbaum.

Gilbert, L. A. (1993). *Two careers, one family: The promise of gender equality.* Newbury Park, CA: Sage.

Gilbert, L. A., & Rachlin, V. (1987). Mental health and psychological functioning of dual-career families. *The Counseling Psychologist, 15,* 7-49.

Glenn, N. D. (1975). The contribution of marriage to the psychological well- being of males and females. *Journal of Marriage and the Family, 37,* 594-601.

Golding, J. M. (1989). Role occupancy and role-specific stress and social support as predictors of depression. *Basic and Applied Social Psychology, 10,* 173-195.

Gore, S., & Mangione, T. W. (1983). Social roles, sex roles and psychological distress: Additive and interactive models of sex differences. *Journal of Health and Social Behavior, 24,* 300-312.

Gottman, G. M., & Potterfield, A. L. (1981). Communicative competence in the nonverbal behavior of married couples. *Journal of Marriage and the Family, 43,* 817-824.

Gove, W. R. (1972). The relationship between sex roles, marital status and mental illness. *Social Forces, 51,* 34-44.

Gove, W. R. (1973). Sex, marital status and mortality. *American Journal of Sociology, 79,* 45-67.

Gove, W. R., & Geerken, M. R. (1977). The effect of children and employment on the mental health of married men and women. *Social Forces, 56,* 66-76.

Gove, W. R., Hughes, M., & Style, C. B. (1983). Does marriage have positive effects on the psychological well-being of the individual? *Journal of Health and Social Behavior, 24,* 122-131.

Gray-Little, B., & Burks, N. (1983). Power and satisfaction in marriage: A review and critique. *Psychological Bulletin, 93,* 513-538.

Greenberger, E., Goldberg, W. A., Crawford, T. J., & Granger, J. (1988). Beliefs about the consequences of marital employment for children. *Psychology of Women Quarterly, 12,* 35-59.

Guarnaccia, P. J., Angel, R., & Worobey, J. L. (1991). The impact of marital status and employment status on depressive affect for Hispanic Americans. *Journal of Community Psychology, 19,* 136-149.

Haas, L. (1986). Wives' orientation toward breadwinning. *Journal of Family Issues, 7,* 358-381.

Hallstrom, T. (1986). Social origins of major depression: The role of provoking agents and vulnerability factors. *Acta Psychiatrica Scandinavica, 73,* 383-389.

Hankin, J. R. (1990). Gender and mental illness. *Research in Community Mental Health, 6,* 183-201.

Haring-Hidore, M., Stock, W. A., Okun, M. A., & Witter, R. A. (1985). Marital status and subjective well-being: A research synthesis. *Journal of Marriage and the Family, 47,* 947-953.

Harris, C., & Earle, J. (1986). Gender and work values: Survey findings from a working-class sample. *Sex Roles, 15,* 487-494.

Hatfield, E., & Rapson, R. L. (1987). Gender differences on love and intimacy: The fantasy vs. the reality. *Journal of Social Work and Human Sexuality, 5*(2), 15-26.

Hawkins, A., Marshall, C., & Meiners, K. (1995). Exploring wives' sense of fairness about family work: An initial test of the distributive justice framework. *Journal of Family Issues, 16,* 693-721.

Heer, D. M. (1962). Husband and wife perceptions of family power structure. *Marriage and Family Living, 24,* 65-67.

Heiss, J. (1988). Women's values regarding marriage and the family. In H. P. McAdoo (Ed.), *Black families* (pp. 201-214). Newbury Park, CA: Sage.

Helgeson, V. S., Shaver, P., & Dyer, M. (1987). Prototypes of intimacy and distance in same-sex and opposite-sex relationships. *Journal of Social and Personal Relationships, 4,* 195-233.

Hochschild, A. (1989). *The second shift: Working parents and the revolution at home.* New York: Viking.

Hoffman, L. (1987). Beyond power and control. *Family Systems Medicine, 3,* 381-396.

Hossain, Z., & Roopnarine, J. L. (1993). Division of household labor and child care in dual-earner African-American families with infants. *Sex Roles, 29,* 571-583.

Howard, J. A., Blumstein, P., & Schwartz, P. (1986). Sex, power and influence tactics in intimate relationships. *Journal of Personality and Social Psychology, 51,* 102-109.

Huber, J., & Spitze, G. (1983). *Sex stratification, children, housework, and jobs.* New York: Academic Press.

Hughes, D., & Galinsky, E. (1994). Gender, job and family conditions, and psychological symptoms. *Psychology of Women Quarterly, 18,* 251-270.

Hunt, J., & Hunt, L. (1987). Male resistance to role symmetry in dual-earner households: Three alternative explanations. In N. Gerstel & H. Gross (Eds.), *Families and work* (pp. 192-203). Philadelphia: Temple University Press.

Huston, T. L. (1983). Power. In H. H. Kelley, E. Bersheid, A. Christensen, J. H. Harvey, T. L. Huston, G. Levinger, E. McClintock, L. A. Peplau, & D. R. Peterson (Eds.), *Close relationships* (pp. 169-219). New York: Freeman.

Instone, D., Major, B., & Bunker, B. (1983). Gender, self confidence, and social influence strategies: An organizational simulation. *Journal of Personality and Social Psychology, 44,* 322-333.

Izraeli, D. N. (1987). Sex effects in the evaluation of influence tactics. *Journal of Occupational Behavior, 8,* 79-86.

John, D., Shelton, B., & Luschen, K. (1995). Race, ethnicity, gender and perceptions of fairness. *Journal of Family Issues, 16,* 357-379.

Johnson, P. B. (1978). Women and interpersonal power. In I. Frieze, J. Parsons, P. Johnson, D. Ruble, & G. Zellman (Eds.), *Women and sex roles: A social psychological perspective* (pp. 302-320). New York: Norton.

Jordan, J. (1986). *The meaning of mutuality.* Wellesley, MA: Wellesley College, Stone Center.

Jump, J., & Haas, L. (1987). Fathers in transition. In M. S. Kimmel (Ed.), *Changing men: New directions in research on men and masculinity* (pp. 98-114). Newbury Park, CA: Sage.

Kaufman, M. (1994). Men, feminism and men's contradictory experiences of power. In H. Brod & M. Kaufman (Eds.), *Theorizing masculinity* (pp. 142-163). Thousand Oaks, CA: Sage.

Kelley, D., & Burgoon, J. (1991). Understanding marital satisfaction and couple type as functions of relational expectations. *Human Communications Research, 18*(1), 40-69.

Kelsoe, J. R., Ginns, E. L., Egeland, J. A., Gerhard, D. S., Goldstein, A. M., Bale, S. J., Pauls, D. L., Long, R. T., Kidd, K. K., Conte, G., Houseman, D. E., & Paul, S. M. (1991). Re-evaluation of the linkage relationship between chromosome 11p loci and the gene for Bipolar Affective Disorder in the old order Amish. In J. A. Talbot, R. J. Frances, D. X. Freeman, H. Y. Meltzer, S. W. Perry, J. E. Schowalter, & S. C. Ydofsky (Eds.), *Yearbook of psychiatry and applied mental health* (pp. 58-59). [Handbook] St. Louis, MO: Mosby Yearbook.

Kessler, R., & McRae, J. (1982). The effect of wives' employment on the mental health of married men and women. *American Sociological Review, 47,* 216-227.

Kessler-Harris, A. (1982). *Out to work: A history of wage earning women in the United States.* New York: Oxford University Press.

Kidder, L., Fagan, M., & Cohn, E. (1981). Giving and receiving: Social justice in close relationships. In M. Lerner & S. Lerner (Eds.), *The justice motive in social behavior: Adapting to times of scarcity and change* (pp. 235-259). New York: Plenum.

King, D. A., & Buchwald, A. M. (1982). Sex differences in subclinical depression: Administration of the Beck Depression Inventory in public and private disclosure situations. *Journal of Personality and Social Psychology, 42,* 963-969.

Kipnis, D., Castell, P. J., Gergen, M., & Mausch, D. (1976). Metamorphic effects of power. *Journal of Applied Psychology, 61,* 127-135.

Kipnis, D., Cohn, E. S., & Catalno, R. (1979, April). *Power and affection.* Paper presented at the Eastern Psychological Association, Philadelphia, PA.

Krafft, S. (1994). Why wives earn less than husbands. *American Demographics, 16*(1), 16-17.

Kranau, E. J., Gree, V., & Valencia-Weber, G. (1982). Acculturation and the Hispanic woman: Attitudes toward women, sex role attribution, sex role behavior, and demographics. *Hispanic Journal of Behavioral Sciences, 4,* 21-40.

Krause, N., & Markides, K. S. (1985). Employment and psychological well-being in Mexican American women. *Journal of Health and Social Behavior, 26,* 15-26.

Krueger, D. L. (1975). Communication patterns and egalitarian decision making in dual-career couples. *Western Journal of Speech Communication, 49,* 126-145.

Labaton, S. (1993, June 17). The man behind the high court nominee. *New York Times,* p. 1.

Lange, S., & Worrell, J. (1990, August). *Satisfaction and commitment in lesbian and heterosexual relationships.* Paper presented at the meeting of the American Psychological Association, Boston, MA.

Lewis, R. A. (1978). Emotional intimacy among men. *Journal of Social Issues, 34,* 108-121.

Lewis, S., Izraeli, D., & Hootsmans, H. (1992). *Dual-earner families: International perspectives.* Newbury Park, CA: Sage.

Lips, H. (1981). *Women, men and power.* Mountain View, CA: Mayfield.

Lynch, J. (1977). *The broken heart: The medical consequences of loneliness.* New York: Basic Books.

Madden, M. E. (1987). Perceived control and power in marriage: A study of marital decision making and task performance. *Personality and Social Psychology Bulletin, 13,* 73-82.

Major, B. (1994). From social inequality to personal entitlement: The role of social comparisons, legitimacy appraisals, and group membership. In M. Zanna (Ed.), *Advances in experimental social psychology* (pp. 293-355). New York: Academic Press.

Malson, M. R. (1983). Black women's sex roles: The social context for a new ideology. *Journal of Social Issues, 39,* 101-113.

Martin, M. (1985). Satisfaction with intimate exchange: Gender-role differences and the impact of equity, equality and rewards. *Sex Roles, 13,* 597-605.

Mason, K. O., & Bumpass, L. L. (1975). Women's sex role ideology. *American Journal of Sociology, 80,* 1212-1219.

Mason, K. O., Czajka, J. L., & Arber, S. (1976). Change in U.S. women's sex-role attitudes, 1964-1974. *American Sociological Review, 41,* 573-596.

Mastekaasa, A. (1995). Age variations in the suicide rates and subjective well-being of married and never-married persons. *Journal of Community and Applied Social Psychology, 5,* 21-39.

McAdams, D. P. (1988). *Power, intimacy, and the life story.* New York: Guilford.

McAdams, D. P., & Bryant, F. B. (1987). Intimacy motivation and subjective mental health in a nationwide sample. *Journal of Personality, 55,* 395-413.

McAdams, D. P., Lester, R. M., Brand, P. A., McNamara, W. J., & Lensky, D. B. (1988). Sex and the TAT: Are women more intimate than men? Do men fear intimacy? *Journal of Personality Assessment, 52,* 397-409.

McAdams, D. P., & Vaillant, G. (1982). Intimacy motivation and psychosocial adjustment: A longitudinal study. *Journal of Personality Assessment, 46,* 586-593.

McClelland, D. (1975). *Power: The inner experience.* New York: Irvington.

Micheals, J., Edwards, J., & Acock, A. (1984). Satisfaction in intimate relationships as a function of inequality, inequity and outcomes. *Social Psychology Quarterly, 47,* 347-357.

Miller, J. B. (1986). *Toward a new psychology of women* (2nd ed.). Boston: Beacon.

Morris, B. (1995, September). Executive women confront midlife crisis. *Fortune,* pp. 60-86.

Murstein, B. I., Cerreto, M., & MacDonald, M. G. (1977). A theory and investigation of the effect of exchange-orientation on marriage and friendship. *Journal of Marriage and the Family, 39,* 543-548.

Nolen-Hoeksema, S. (1987). Sex differences in unipolar depression: Evidence and theory. *Psychological Bulletin, 101,* 259-282.

Nolen-Hoeksema, S. (1990). *Sex differences in depression.* Stanford, CA: Stanford University Press.

Noller, P. (1980). Misunderstandings in marital communication: A study of couples' nonverbal communication. *Journal of Personality and Social Psychology, 39,* 1135-1148.

Norton, A., & Moorman, J. (1987). Current trends in marriage and divorce among American women. *Journal of Marriage and the Family, 49,* 3-14.

Nyquist, L., Slivken, K., Spence, J., & Helmreich, R. L. (1985). Household responsibilities in middle-class couples: The contribution of demographic and personality variables. *Sex Roles, 12,* 15-34.

Oakley, A. (1974). *Women's work: The housewife, past and present.* New York: Pantheon.

Parry, G. (1987). Sex-role beliefs, work attitudes and mental health in employed and non-employed mothers. *British Journal of Social Psychology, 20,* 47-58.

Pearlin, L. I., & Johnson, J. S. (1977). Marital status, life-strains and depression. *American Sociological Review, 42,* 704-715.

Pennebaker, J. W., & Beale, S. K. (1986). Confronting a traumatic event: Toward an understanding of inhibition and disease. *Journal of Abnormal Psychology, 95*(3), 274-281.

Pennebaker, J. W., Colder, M., & Sharp, L. K. (1990). Accelerating the coping process. *Journal of Personality and Social Psychology, 58*, 528-537.

Pennebaker, J. W., Hughes, C. F., & O'Heeron, R. C. (1987). The psychophysiology of confession: Linking inhibitory and psychosomatic process. *Journal of Personality and Social Psychology, 52*, 781-793.

Pennebaker, J. W., Kiecolt-Glaser, J., & Glaser, R. (1988). Disclosure of traumas and immune function: Health implications for psychotherapy. *Journal of Consulting and Clinical Psychology, 56*, 239-245.

Peplau, L. A. (1983). Roles and gender. In H. H. Kelley, E. Berscheid, A. Christensen, J. H. Harvey, T. L. Huston, G. Levinger, E. McClintock, L. A. Peplau, & D. R. Peterson (Eds.), *Close relationships* (pp. 220-264). New York: Freeman.

Perry-Jenkins, M., & Crouter, A. C. (1990). Men's provider-role attitudes: Implications for household work and marital satisfaction. *Journal of Family Issues, 11*, 136-156.

Perry-Jenkins, M., Seery, B., & Crouter, A. C. (1992). Linkages between women's provider-role attitudes, psychological well-being, and family relationships. *Psychology of Women Quarterly, 16*, 311-329.

Phillips, D. L., & Segal, B. E. (1969). Sexual status and psychiatric symptoms. *American Sociological Review, 34*, 58-72.

Pleck, J. H. (1985). *Working wives, working husbands.* Beverly Hills, CA: Sage.

Potuchek, J. (1992). Employed wives' orientations to breadwinning: A gender theory analysis. *Journal of Marriage and the Family, 54*, 548-558.

Prager, K. J. (1995). *The psychology of intimacy.* New York: Guilford.

President's Commission on Mental Health. (1978). *Report of the subpanel on mental health of women* (No. PEMP/P-78/14). Springfield, VA: National Information Service, U.S. Department of Commerce.

Puglieski, K. (1988). Employment characteristics, social support, and the well-being of women. *Women and Health, 14*(1), 35-38.

Radloff, L. (1975). Sex differences in depression: The effects of occupation and marital status. *Sex Roles, 1*, 249-265.

Rajecki, D. W., Bledsoe, S. B., & Rasmussen, J. L. (1991). Successful personal ads: Gender differences and similarities in offers, stipulations and outcomes. *Basic and Applied Social Psychology, 12*, 457-469.

Raven, B. (1974). The comparative analysis of power and power preference. In J. T. Tedeschi (Ed.), *Perspectives on social power* (pp. 172-200). Chicago: Aldine.

Raven, B. H., Centers, R., & Rodrigues, A. (1975). The basis of conjugal power. In R. E. Cromwell & D. H. Olsen (Eds.), *Power in families* (pp. 217-234). Beverly Hills, CA: Sage.

Raven, B. H., & Kruglanski, A. W. (1970). Conflict in power. In P. Swingle (Ed.), *The structure of conflict* (pp. 69-109). New York: Academic Press.

Ray, J. (1990). Interactional patterns and marital satisfaction among dual-career couples. *Journal of Independent Social Work, 4*(3), 61-73.

Reis, H. T. (1990). The role of intimacy in interpersonal relations. *Journal of Social and Clinical Psychology, 9,* 15-30.

Reis, H. T., Senchak, M., & Solomon, B. (1985). Sex differences in the intimacy of social interaction: Further examination of potential explanations. *Journal of Personality and Social Psychology, 48,* 1204-1217.

Reis, H. T., & Shaver, P. (1988). Intimacy as an interpersonal process. In S. W. Duck (Ed.), *Handbook of personal relationships* (pp. 367-391). New York: John Wiley & Sons.

Reisman, J. M. (1990). Intimacy in same-sex friendships. *Sex Roles, 23,* 65-82.

Repetti, R. L., Matthews, K. A., & Waldron, I. (1989). Employment and women's health. *American Psychologist, 44,* 1394-1401.

Rose, S. (1985). Same- and cross-sex friendships and the psychology of homosexuality. *Sex Roles, 12,* 63-74.

Rosenbluth, S. (in press). Is sexual relationship orientation a matter of choice? *Psychology of Women Quarterly.*

Rosenbluth, S., & Steil, J. (1995). Predictors of intimacy for women in heterosexual and homosexual couples. *Journal of Social and Personal Relationships, 12,* 163-175.

Rosenbluth, S., Steil, J., & Whitcomb, J. (under revision). Marital equality: What does it mean? *Journal of Family Issues.*

Ross, C. E., & Mirowsky, J. (1988). Child care and emotional adjustment to wives' employment. *Journal of Health and Social Behavior, 29,* 127-138.

Ross, C. E., Mirowsky, J., & Huber, J. (1983). Dividing work, sharing work, and in-between: Marriage patterns and depression. *American Sociological Review, 48,* 809-823.

Ross, C. E., Mirowsky, J., & Ulbrich, P. (1983). Distress and the traditional female role: A comparison of Mexicans and Anglos. *American Journal of Sociology, 89,* 670-682.

Rubin, L. (1983). *Intimate strangers: Men and women together.* New York: Harper Perennial Library.

Russo, N. F. (1990). Overview: Forging research priorities for women's mental health. *American Psychologist, 45,* 368-373.

Safilios-Rothschild, C. (1969). Family sociology or wives' family sociology? A cross cultural examination of decision making. *Journal of Marriage and the Family, 31,* 290-301.

Sapadin, L. A. (1988). Friendship and gender: Perspectives of professional men and women. *Journal of Social and Personal Relationships, 5,* 387-403.

Scanzoni, J. (1972). *Sexual bargaining: Power politics in the American marriage.* Englewood Cliffs, NJ: Prentice Hall.

Scanzoni, J. (1975). Sex roles, economic factors, and marital solidarity in Black and White marriages. *Journal of Marriage and the Family, 37,* 130-144.

Scanzoni, J. (1979). Sex role influences on married women's status attainments. *Journal of Marriage and the Family, 41,* 793-800.

Scanzoni, J., & Szinovacz, M. (1980). *Family decision making: A developmental sex role model.* Beverly Hills, CA: Sage.

Scarr, S., Phillips, D., & McCartney, K. (1989). Working mothers and their families. *American Psychologist, 44,* 1402-1409.

Schaeffer, M. T., & Olson, D. H. (1981). Assessing intimacy: The pair inventory. *Journal of Marital and Family Therapy, 7,* 47-60.

Secord, P., & Ghee, K. (1986). Implications of the Black marriage market for marital conflict. *Journal of Family Issues, 1,* 21-30.

Sexton, R. E., & Sexton V. S. (1982). Intimacy: A historical perspective. In M. Fisher & G. Stricker, (Eds.), *Intimacy* (pp. 1-20). New York: Plenum.

Sholomskas, D., & Axelrod, R. (1986). The influence of mother-daughter relationships on women's sense of self and current role choices. *Psychology of Women Quarterly, 10,* 171-182.

Silberstein, L. (1992). *Dual-career marriage: A system in transition.* Hillsdale, NJ: Lawrence Erlbaum.

Solomon, Z., & Bromet, E. (1982). The role of social factors in affective disorder: An assessment of the vulnerability model of Brown and his colleagues. *Psychological Medicine, 12,* 123-130.

South, S. (1993). Racial and ethnic differences in the desire to marry. *Journal of Marriage and the Family, 55,* 357-370.

Spitze, G. (1988). Women's employment and family relations: A review. *Journal of Marriage and the Family, 50,* 595-618.

Steil, J. M. (1983). Marriage: An unequal partnership. In B. Wolman & G. Stricker (Eds.), *Handbook of family and marital therapy* (pp. 49-60). New York: Plenum.

Steil, J. M. (1984). Marital relationships and mental health: The psychic costs of inequality. In J. Freeman (Ed.), *Women: A feminist perspective* (3rd ed.) (pp. 113-123). Palo Alto, CA: Mayfield.

Steil, J. M. (1994). Equality and entitlement in marriage. In M. Lerner & G. Mikula (Eds.), *Entitlement and the affectional bond* (pp. 229-258). New York: Plenum.

Steil, J. M., & Hillman, J. (1993). Perceived value of direct and indirect influence strategies: A cross cultural perspective. Special issue on cross cultural perspectives. *Psychology of Women Quarterly, 17,* 457-462.

Steil, J. M., & Makowski, D. (1989). Equity, equality and need: A study of the patterns and outcomes associated with their use in intimate relationships. *Social Justice Research, 3,* 121-137.

Steil, J. M., Smrz, A., Wilkens, C., & Barnett, R. (1995, August). *Why is relationship equality so hard to achieve?* Symposium conducted at the Conference of the International Network on Personal Relationships, Williamsburg, VA.

Steil, J. M., & Turetsky, B. (1987a). Is equal better? The relationship between marital equality and psychological symptomatology. In S. Oskamp (Ed.), *Applied social psychology annual* (pp. 73-95). Newbury Park, CA: Sage.

Steil, J. M., & Turetsky, B. (1987b). Marital influence levels and symptomatology among wives. In F. Crosby (Ed.), *Spouse parent worker: On gender and multiple roles* (pp. 74-90). New Haven, CT: Yale University Press.

Steil, J. M., & Weltman, K. (1991). Marital inequality: The importance of resources, personal attributes, and social norms on career valuing and domestic influence. *Sex Roles, 24,* 161-179.

Steil, J. M., & Weltman, K. (1992). Influence strategies at home and at work: A study of sixty dual career couples. *Journal of Social and Personal Relationships, 9,* 65-88.

Steil, J. M., & Whitcomb, J. (1992, July). *Conceptualizations of inequality.* Paper presented at the Sixth International Conference on Personal Relationships, University of Maine, Orono, ME.

Stroebe, M. S., & Stroebe, W. (1983). Who suffers more? Sex differences in health risks of the widowed. *Psychological Bulletin, 93,* 279-301.

Taylor, J., Henderson, D., & Jackson, B. B. (1991). A holistic model for understanding and predicting depressive symptoms in African-American women. *Journal of Community Psychology, 19,* 306-320.

Taylor, R., Chatters, L., Tucker, M., & Lewis, E. (1990). Developments in research on black families: A decade review. *Journal of Marriage and the Family, 52,* 993-1014.

Thoits, P. A. (1985). Social support and psychological well-being: Theoretical possibilities. In I. Sarason & B. Sarason (Eds.), *Social support: Theory, research and applications* (pp. 51-72). Dordrecht, The Netherlands: Martinus Nijhoff.

Thoits, P. A. (1986). Multiple identities: Examining gender and marital status differences in distress. *American Sociological Review, 51,* 259-272.

Thompson, L., & Walker, A. J. (1989). Gender in families: Women and men in marriage, work and parenthood. *Journal of Marriage and the Family, 51,* 845-871.

Tschann, J. M. (1988). Self-disclosure in adult friendship: Gender and marital status differences. *Journal of Social and Personal Relationships, 5,* 65-81.

Turk, J. L., & Bell, N. W. (1972). Measuring power in families. *Journal of Marriage and the Family, 34,* 215-233.

Ulbrich, P. M. (1988). The determinants of depression in two-income marriages. *Journal of Marriage and the Family, 50,* 121-131.

U.S. Bureau of the Census. (1995a). *Current population reports: Population characteristics, marital status and living arrangements.* Washington, DC: U. S. Government Printing Office.

U.S. Bureau of the Census. (1995b). *Statistical abstract of the United States: 1995.* Washington, DC: U. S. Government Printing Office.

VanFossen, B. E. (1981). Sex differences in the mental health effects of spouse support and equity. *Journal of Health and Social Behavior, 22,* 130-143.

VanFossen, B. E. (1986). Sex differences in depression: The role of spouse support. In S. E. Hobfoll (Ed.), *Stress, social support and women* (pp. 69-84). New York: Hemisphere.

Vannoy-Hiller, D., & Philliber, W. W. (1989). *Equal partners: Successful women in marriage.* Newbury Park, CA: Sage.

VanYperen, N., & Buunk, B. (1990). A longitudinal study of equity and satisfaction in intimate relationships. *European Journal of Social Psychology, 20,* 287-309.

VanYperen, N., & Buunk, B. (1991). Sex-role attitudes, social comparison and relationship satisfaction. *Social Psychology Quarterly, 54,* 169-180.

Veroff, J., Douvan, E., & Kulka, R. A. (1981). *The inner American: A self portrait from 1957 to 1976.* New York: Basic Books.

Veroff, J., Kulka, R., & Douvan, E. (1981). *Mental health in America: Patterns of help seeking.* New York: Basic Books.

Waldron, I., & Jacobs, J. A. (1989). Effects of multiple roles on women's health—evidence from a national longitudinal study. *Women and Health, 15*(1), 3-19.

Walster, E., Walster, G. W., & Berscheid, E. (1978). *Equity: Theory and research.* Boston: Allyn & Bacon.

Waltz, M., Badura, B., Pfaff, H., & Schott, T. (1988). Marriage and the psychological consequences of a heart attack: A longitudinal study of the adaptation to chronic illness after 3 years. *Social Science Medicine, 27,* 149-158.

Waring, E. M., Patton, D., Neron, C. A., & Linker, W. (1986). Types of marital intimacy and prevalence of emotional illness. *Canadian Journal of Psychiatry, 31,* 720-726.

Waring, E. M., Tillman, M. P., Frelick, L., Russell, L., & Weisz, G. (1980). Concepts of intimacy in the general population. *Journal of Nervous and Mental Disease, 168,* 471-474.

Warr, P., & Parry, G. (1982). Paid employment and women's psychological well-being. *Psychological Bulletin, 91,* 498-516.

Weingarten, K. (1978). The employment pattern of professional couples and their distribution of involvement in the family. *Psychology of Women Quarterly, 3,* 43-52.

Weiss, R. S. (1987). Men and their wives' work. In F. Crosby (Ed.) *Spouse, parent, worker: On gender and multiple roles* (pp. 109-121). New Haven, CT: Yale University Press.

Weissman, M., & Klerman, G. (1977). Sex differences and the epidemiology of depression. *Archives of General Psychiatry, 34,* 98-111.

Weissman, M., & Paykel, E. (1974). *The depressed woman: A study of social relationships.* Chicago: University of Chicago Press.

Wetzel, J. (1990). American families: 75 years of change. *Monthly Labor Review, 113,* 4-13.

White, J. W., & Roufail, M. (1989). Gender and influence strategies of first choice and last resort. *Psychology of Women Quarterly, 13,* 175-189.

White, K. M., Speisman, J. C., Jackson, D., Bartis, S., & Costos, D. (1986). Intimacy maturity and its correlates in young married couples. *Journal of Personality and Social Psychology, 50,* 152-162.

Wilkie, J. (1993). Changes in U.S. men's attitudes toward the family provider role, 1972-1989. *Gender & Society, 7,* 261-279.

Williamson, G., & Clark, M. (1989). The communal/exchange distinction and some implications for understanding justice in families. *Social Justice Research, 3,* 77-103.

Wood, W., Rhodes, N., & Whelen, M. (1989). Sex differences in positive well-being: A consideration of emotional style and marital status. *Psychological Bulletin, 106,* 249-264.

Wynne, L. C., & Wynne, A. R. (1986). The quest for intimacy. *Journal of Marital and Family Therapy, 12,* 383-394.

Yankelovich, D. (1974). The meaning of work. In J. M. Resow (Ed.), *The worker and the job: Coping with change* (pp. 19-47). Englewood Cliffs, NJ: Prentice Hall.

Yogev, S. (1987). Marital satisfaction and sex role perceptions among dual-earner couples. *Journal of Social and Personal Relationships, 9,* 35-45.

Zeitz, B. (1981). *Corporations and two-career families: Directions for the future.* New York: Catalyst Career and Family Center.

Name Index

Subject Index

About the Author

Janice M. Steil is Professor of Psychology at the Derner Institute of Advanced Psychological Studies at Adelphi University. Trained as a social psychologist, she received her PhD from Columbia University in 1979. Her research interests include the psychology of justice and issues of justice and well-being in close relationships. She is currently an associate editor of *Psychology of Women Quarterly*.